I0781329

Organized Action

A Symbolic Interactionist Synthesis of
George Herbert Mead and Max Weber

Gerald Dea Morris

Organized Action

Gerald Dea Morris

Published by:
Gerald Dea Morris, Ph.D.
The Mead–Weber Synthesis Project
Portland, 97206 OR, USA

Typesetting & Cover Design: Sara Morris

ISBN: 9781723920479

Imprint: Independently published.

Printed in USA.

This essay is dedicated to Alex Garber,
professor, mentor, friend.

Human society is to be seen as consisting of acting people, and the life of the society is to be seen as consisting of their actions. The acting units may be separate individuals, collectivities whose members are acting together on a common quest, or organizations acting on behalf of a constituency. Whatever be the acting unit - an individual, a family, a school, a church, a business firm, a labor union, a legislature, and so on - any particular action is formed in the light of the situation in which it takes place. This leads to the recognition of a second major condition, namely, that the action is formed or constructed by interpreting the situation. Such interpretative behavior may take place in the individual guiding his own action, in a collectivity of individuals acting in concert, or in "agents" acting on behalf of a group or organization.

—**Herbert Blumer,** *Society as Symbolic Interaction*, **1960**

Contents

Preface

When I left university I took a position with the American Federation of Teachers, the organization I had studied in my Ph.D. thesis. With my social science background I was soon invited to do policy work relating to the AFT's federal legislative program. Over the next two decades I worked closely with lobbyists in the AFT and in many other education and labor organizations. This involved spending a great amount of time on the Hill, in the Capitol, in committee rooms, in legislators' offices, and at congressional receptions.

In time, I observed that a small number of lobbyists were extraordinarily adept in "taking the attitude of the other" with respect to members of Congress. They didn't miss cues as to what was happening, they could anticipate the responses of legislators, and they were able to effectively communicate. This demonstrated a deep understanding of the thinking of congressional members. In contrast, many advocates on the Hill had difficulty mentally "stepping into the shoes" of a legislator. This observation, and others like it, led me to continually invoke the ideas of George Herbert Mead in my work.

Similarly, when I was working on a large and complex legislative matter, I began to notice patterns in the support and opposition to the legislation. I was standing outside the House chamber, near the elevators, where many lobbyists stand, sorting out in my mind the constituencies for and against different aspects of the legislation. As I was doing this inventory, it suddenly occurred to me that the breakdown, the categories I was using, were versions of Weber's "class," "status group," and "party." From that point on, I observed that Weber's concepts were invaluable in sorting out—and most especially in testing—ideas about the struggle over any piece of legislation.

Legislative work on the Hill was an excellent laboratory in which to mold and test ideas with respect to a synthesis of Mead and Weber's concepts. In doing so, I was responding to a challenge put to me by Alex Garber, my former professor, who had studied under Herbert Blumer, at Chicago and at Berkeley, and under Reinhardt Bendix, at Berkeley. A long time ago, he said undertaking this essay would be a very worthwhile endeavor. It gives me great pleasure to complete this manuscript and dedicate it to the memory of Alex Garber, who introduced me to Mead and Weber.

CHAPTER I.

Primary Colors

In the world of visual arts there are colors designated as "primary colors." With regard to human vision these colors are elemental. Images viewed in motion pictures, film and computer animation, magazine photographs, wall posters, and such, all rely on combinations of primary colors. Blended in various ways the primary colors produce a great variety of other colors. In fact, they produce all of the colors that humans can see. The additional colors are often called "secondary" or "tertiary" colors. Generally three in number, the primary colors are distinctions that humans recognize within a continuous spectrum of light. Historically the primary colors commonly recognized were red, yellow, and blue. And, this selection is still widely used today. The concept that a set of primary colors may be mixed to produce all other visible colors is, in itself, valid. However, red, yellow, and blue are not, for most purposes, the best selection of primary colors. The red, yellow, blue selection predates modern scientific study, which has determined that other primary color combinations are more accurate, more complete. Using a traditional pallet of red, yellow, and blue does not allow one to produce a full range of visible colors. Accordingly, in modern applications different primary color combinations are more frequently used.

Depending upon the application, the primary colors work by addition—that is, by combining their separate qualities—or by subtraction—that is, by blocking other colors. The standard primary colors used in the additive process are red, green and blue. This is called the "RGB model" of primary colors. Applications such as television and computer screens use the RGB additive process. They start with a dark background and add combinations of red, green, and blue light to produce an image. The standard colors used in the subtractive process are cyan, magenta, and yellow—with black added to give tonality. This is called the "CMYK model," with K representing black. However, what one ultimately recognizes is combinations of red, green, and blue. The CMYK model is used in applications such as commercial printing. Unlike the additive process, which starts with a dark background, the subtractive process ordinarily starts with a light background, say a white piece of paper. In addition to allowing the reflection of desired colors, the CMYK pigments block the reflection of unwanted colors from the light background.

Regardless of the means by which they are produced, the colors red, green, and blue are the colors fundamental to human vision. The physical structure of the human eye is such that red, green, and blue—or combinations thereof—are the colors ordinarily seen. As stated, all other colors of the visible light spectrum can be produced by adding different combinations of these three colors. Mixed together in equal amounts, red, green, and blue light will produce white light. Absent these colors, there will be no visible light at all. Now, white light can be separated into the primary colors or, as the case may be, into a mixture of the primary colors. This is ordinarily done by glass prisms, distortions in glass windows, droplets of water in the atmosphere, oil slicks on water, and other refractive means. So, why discuss primary colors in this essay on organizations and social theory? The primary colors offer a useful analogy for the composition of social action. Just as various colors are composed of the three primary colors, any social action can be seen as a blend of three primary types of action. More properly, every social action conveys three primary meanings of action. And, just as light can be separated into its component primary colors, human social action can be conceptually separated into its component types of action. Whereas the components of light are displayed by optical means, the three qualities of social action are displayed by means of analytic concepts. By means of special concepts, the qualitatively different threads in the fabric of social action can be pulled apart and examined.

When speaking of social action in a broad and inclusive manner, individuals frequently refer to the "economic," "social," and "political" makeup of such action. Society as a whole is tacitly summarized by referring to these three modes of social action. As the following examples illustrate, notable individuals often make such comments in their public speaking and writing (sources listed in Bibliography):

» Rosa Luxemburg, speaking on the Russo-Japanese War, said in 1904:

The war completely rends all the veils which the bourgeoisie world—this world of economic, political and social fetishism—constantly wraps us in.

» President Theodore Roosevelt suggested in 1910:

We ought to use the National Government as an agency, a tool, whenever it is necessary, in order that we may organize our entire political, economic and social life in accordance with a far-reaching democratic purpose.

» General Douglas McArthur included, in reference to post-war Japan, in his 1951 farewell address to Congress:

Politically, economically, and socially, Japan is now abreast of many free nations of the earth and will not again fail the universal trust.

» President Dwight Eisenhower, upon nominating Earl Warren as Chief Justice of the Supreme Court in 1953, remarked:

He represents the kind of political, economic, and social thinking that I believe we need on the Supreme Court.

» Pope John XXIII, taking a stand for worker rights in 1961, asserted:

We would observe, finally, that the present demand for workers to have a greater say in the conduct of the firm accords not only with man's nature, but also with recent progress in the economic, social, and political system.

» Malcolm X took a militant stance in 1964 by proclaiming:

We suffer political oppression, economic exploitation, and social degradation, all of them from the same enemy.

» Martin Luther King stated in a speech in 1964:

Power properly understood is nothing but the ability to achieve purpose. It is the strength required to bring about social, political and economic change.

> » Aung San Sun Ky, Nobel Laureate, professed at an international forum in 1995:

The struggle for democracy and human rights is a struggle for life and dignity. It is a struggle that encompasses our political, social and economic aspirations.

> » Emma Watson, actor and UN Goodwill Ambassador, declared in 2014:

For the record, feminism by definition is: "The belief that men and women should have equal rights and opportunities. It is the theory of the political, economic and social equality of the sexes."

> » Presidential candidate Hillary Clinton said in 2016:

We face a complex set of economic, social, and political challenges. They are intersectional, they are reinforcing, and we have got to take them all on.

This list could be expanded, seemingly without limit, for references to political, social, and economic action as a totality are ubiquitous. This essay will suggest that it is not simply a matter of convention or phraseology that notable individuals often refer in summary fashion to the economic, social, and political aspects of society or social action. Comments such as those cited above appear to recognize intuitively what are recurrent patterns in social action. The choice of language reflects what may be called the primary colors, or qualitative dimensions, of all social action. In their speaking and writing, individuals make these distinctions because they seem to fit with experience. They seem to make sense. Social action, as a whole, is viewed as a composite of economic, social, and political patterns of action. (Later this essay will posit, more generally and in parallel terms, that all social action has objective, subjective, and dominance aspects.)

Scholars have frequently made note of the economic, social, and political makeup of social action. Even Karl Marx, known to give primacy to economic factors in social action, recognized the importance of the political and social dimensions of society (1977, passim). He envisioned a political and social superstructure in society based on an economic substructure. Max Weber, of particular importance to this essay, expanded on Marx and gave a balanced consideration to the economic, social, and political dimensions in society (Bendix, 1960, p.286). This recognition was foundational in his wide-ranging analysis of social phenomena. Depending upon the particular analytic context he used different terms, but nonetheless made comparable distinctions.

Daniel Bell, a leading intellectual of the Twentieth Century and Harvard professor, had a similar analysis. Bell identified three realms within society: "techno-economic," "cultural," and "polity." He used these qualitative distinctions extensively in his analysis of social action:

> *Almost all of contemporary social science thinks of society as some unified "system," organized around some single major principle… It is my belief, on the other hand, that one can best analyze modern society by thinking of it as an uneasy amalgam of three distinct realms: the social structure (principally the techno-economic order), the polity, and the culture. (1996, p.xxx)*

Bell continues:

> *The social structure comprises the economy, technology, and the occupational system. The polity regulates the distribution of power and adjudicates the conflicting claims and demands of individuals and groups. The culture is the realm of expressive symbolism and meanings. (1973, p.12)*

Bell suggests each realm in a society, in a particular epoch, has a distinctive "axial," or central, principle (1973, p.12). In addition to speaking of realms, Bell sometimes uses the terms "dimensions," "orders," or "estates" (p.115; p.487). He also mentions three types of organizations, "political," "economic," and "social" (p.119). This differentiation of political, economic, and social organizations will be of importance later in this essay.

George Herbert Mead, the author other than Weber of principal importance in this essay, also recognized three types of action expressed "very early" in human society. In discussing these "universals" of human behavior, Mead identifies three types of attitudes toward others in social interaction (1965a, p.281–284). One is "neighborliness," which underlies, for example, religious behavior; another is an "economic" orientation, which arises from a process of material exchange; and the third is a "political" orientation, which begins as "dominance" and develops into an "administrative" orientation. Enabling these universals is a universal of "discourse." For the purposes of this essay neighborliness, economic, and political/administrative orientations are taken to be synonymous with social, economic, and political distinctions. In addition, the terms cultural and social are largely interchangeable in referring to a group's collectively held ideas—"beliefs," "values," "norms"—plus the cohesive behavior that is oriented to expressing and sharing such ideas.

This essay explores the three dimensions of action in several contexts and at several levels of analysis. It will have three principal objectives:

» It will outline a perspective that integrates, or synthesizes, key theoretical ideas of George Herbert Mead and Max Weber.

» It will present an approach to "symbolic interactionism," a sociological paradigm based on Mead's ideas, as a method to analyze large social structures or events.

» It will suggest a way of melding diverse theories about "complex organizations" into a unified perspective.

As to the last point, above, why study complex organizations? In reply, one could say that historically complex organizations are one of human society's greatest inventions. With complex organization one can put a large number of people together in a common endeavor, consciously relate the means and ends of group action, and accomplish tasks well beyond the capacity of individuals or simple groups. Large, complex organizations have been responsible for some of humankind's greatest achievements—space exploration, CERN, medical research, etc. Large, complex organizations have also been essential to some of humankind's worst achievements, such as Nazi, Fascist, Stalinist and similar forms of dominance. Nonetheless, without large, complex organizations it is hard to imagine how modern civilization could proceed. Such organizations are omnipresent in today's society: national, state, and local governments; national and global business corporations; great research universities; mega churches; NGOs of every imaginable type, and so forth. For the purpose of this essay, analyzing complex organizations will demonstrate the viability of symbolic interactionism in dealing with large social structures or events.

Unfortunately, as a scholarly field, complex organization is notably fragmented. There are frequent complaints about a lack of unity among the many organizational theories. One only need look at a standard college textbook for a survey course on complex organizations. The table of contents will likely reveal a multiplicity of competing theories. Probing deeper, one may discover there is even scant agreement on how to define what is, or is not, an organization. Lex Donaldson, a highly regarded theorist, states there is a "proliferation of paradigms" and a lack of unity in organizational theory. He concludes, "This plurality of paradigms fragments the field and prevents the cumulation of knowledge.

Attempts at synthesis to date have been less than completely successful" (1995, p.31). And, each of the numerous paradigms, or theories, offers only a partial vision of organized group action. Donaldson observes, "Each of the paradigms is itself limited and flawed" (p.5).

This essay will suggest that the diversity of organizational theories is similar to the old story of the three blind men and an elephant. The story goes somewhat as follows. Upon approaching the elephant the first blind man felt its leg and said the elephant was like a tree. The second blind man grasped the elephant's tail and said it was like a snake. The third blind man put his hand upon the elephant's side and said it was like a wall. This essay will propose that much of the divergence among organizational theories depends upon which organizational dimension—economic, social, or political—is viewed as central, or perhaps considered exclusively. In addition, it will outline a synthesis of organizational theory based on the social-psychology of George Herbert Mead and the sociology of Max Weber, a synthesis that balances consideration of the three dimensions.

With regard to the second objective of presenting symbolic interactionism as a methodology for analyzing large social structures and events, this responds to a long-standing criticism in the sociological literature. A number of scholars have stated that symbolic interactionism, an otherwise compelling perspective, is of little use beyond analysis of simple, interpersonal interactions. But first, what is meant by symbolic interactionism? In this essay the term refers to the legacy of George Herbert Mead and his principal student, Herbert Blumer. The substance of this perspective will be clarified throughout the essay, however it is generally known as the Chicago School of symbolic interactionism.

Within the fold of symbolic interactionism, the Chicago School, in particular, has frequently been criticized for failing to deal adequately with large social structures. C. Wright Mills notes the failure of symbolic interactionism to analyze the "broader context" of "interpersonal relations" (1961, p.160). According to Ashley Crossman (2017), "Critics of this theory claim that symbolic interactionism neglects the macro level of social interpretation—the big picture." Pascale relates that he found the perspective "has some trouble getting at routine relations of power" and was "unable to analyze race, class, power, and ability as routine relations of power and privilege" (2010, p.103). Stryker states, "Mead's concept of 'generalized other' erases distinctions among social structures within societies despite variations consequential for social interaction" (1981, p.18). Stryker's comment about the "generalized other" refers to a central concept in Mead's theory. Nonetheless, this essay will argue that outlining a synthesis of Mead and

Weber's ideas will make explicit a symbolic interactionist approach to social structure, particularly as illustrated in the case of large, complex organizations.

As to the first objective, outlining a synthesis of the key theoretical ideas of Mead and Weber, this task will necessarily underlie the other two objectives of the essay. In bringing together the perspectives of Mead and Weber, the essay will explore a fundamental theoretical kinship that has often been suggested in sociological literature. For example, Teryakian states that key ideas in symbolic interactionism were borrowed by Mead from Weber's core concept of *verstehen* (1965, p.679). Cohen speaks of "the complimentary influences of Weberian sociology and Median social psychology" (1985, p.72). Pascale observes, "In addition to Weber, the philosophical school of pragmatism profoundly influenced the development of symbolic interactionism" (2010, p.78). Mead, of course, was one of the leading pragmatist philosophers. Crossman (2017) comments as follows:

> *Although symbolic interactionism traces its origins to Max Weber's assertion that individuals act according to their interpretation of the meaning of their world, the American philosopher George Herbert Mead introduced this perspective to American sociology in the 1920s.*

Gerth and Mills, who translated important writings by Weber, refer to, "The pragmatic view of ideas, which Max Weber shares with Karl Marx and John Dewey" (Weber, 1946, p.65). Dewey was Mead's closest associate, and what is said of Dewey in this context could easily be said of Mead, as well. Finally, Bordieu adds:

> *The fact that it would not be difficult to extract the explicitly stated principles of a theory of symbolic interaction from Weber's theoretical writings makes the reformulation of Weberian analysis in the language of symbolic interaction all the easier and, it would seem, all the more legitimate. (2008, p.121)*

This essay will argue that a synthesis of the theories of Mead and Weber offers the prospect of a powerful symbolic interactionist perspective and qualitative methodology. What follows is an attempt to outline a synthesis, however it does not claim to present the ideas of either theorist in a comprehensive manner.

CHAPTER II

George Herbert Mead

At this point a brief exposition of George Herbert Mead's social psychology is in order. Mead lived from February 27, 1863, to April 26, 1931. He and Max Weber were contemporaries, although the two apparently never met. Mead was a major pragmatist philosopher and taught at the University of Chicago. A close associate of John Dewey, who was instrumental in bringing him to the University of Chicago, he is known for his contributions to both philosophy and social psychology. The centerpiece of Mead's work is a theory of human intelligence and how the individual human "mind" is formed in society. Said otherwise, his main interest was the social genesis of the human "self," or personality. Thus, Charles Morris states in the introduction to Mead's most influential book, *Mind, Self, and Society*:

> *In many ways the most secure and imposing result of pragmatic activity to date has been its theory of intelligence and mind. Such a theory is, of course, basic to the whole structure. The development and elaboration of this theory defines the life- long activity of George H. Mead. (Mead, 1965a, p.x)*

In Mead's view the individual self, or personality, emerges and develops as a product of social interaction. And, as a social construction it mirrors the social relations in which it develops. In this sense, the self is a microcosm of society. Mead says, "The unity and structure of the complete self reflects the unity and structure of the social process as a whole" (p.144). More specifically, the individual self arises through social interaction in a language community. Absent such experience, the human mind, or intelligence, would not emerge and develop. Again, Charles Morris states, "Mead's endeavor is to show that mind and the self are without residue social emergents; and that language, in the form of the vocal gesture, provides the mechanism for their emergence" (p.xiv).

According to Mead an essential for the emergence of the individual personality, or self, is the development and use of "significant symbols" (p.71–74). The language used by a community is simply a collection of significant symbols. Technically, a significant symbol is an action that arouses in the maker the same response as in the recipient. To give a simple example, if one spontaneously shouts "fire" upon being confronted by a perceived threat, one likely responds to this shout much the same as do nearby others. Or, one may carelessly say something and then in embarrassment say to oneself, "Oh my, did I really say that?" At the same time, others may be expected to have a similar response, "Did he actually say that?" In human society, significant symbols provide the means of social interaction. It is through the use of significant symbols that an individual signals the intent (i.e., meaning) of his or her behavior and anticipates the behavior of others. That is, mentally, one plays both sides of an interaction. Through the agency of significant symbols one can converse with others, engage in joint actions, or interact and have a conversation with oneself. By dint of significant symbols one can mentally stand outside of oneself, objectify oneself, see one's action from the perspectives of others, mentally test possible actions, and thereby exercise self direction. Charles Morris remarks about significant symbols, "Through their use the individual is 'taking the role of the other' in the regulation of his own conduct" (p.xxi).

What is called thinking, or reasoning, is an internal form of social interaction. Charles Morris sums up Mead's perspective on the individual mind, "It is the internalization within the individual of the social process of communication in which meaning emerges" (p.xxii). Thus, when thinking, even when completely alone, one is socially engaged. This is no less true of scientific thought, or of artistic creativity, than it is of personal reasoning. In the process of thinking one imaginatively interacts with oneself as a social object. Mead says, "When you are reasoning you are indicating to yourself the characters that call out certain responses—and that is all you are doing" (p.93). Said otherwise, in the process of thinking one is acting as both subject and object. According to Charles Morris, "Mead finds the distinguishing trait of selfhood to reside in the capacity of the minded organism to be an object to itself" (p.xxiii). In Mead's own words, "The self, as that which can be an object to itself, is essentially a social structure, and it arises in social experience" (p.140).

Mead describes the symbolic process of being an object to oneself, of taking, or assuming, the attitudes of others toward oneself, in terms of the "I" and the "me." More specifically, "The 'I' reacts to the self which arises through the taking of the attitudes of 'Others,' through taking those attitudes one has introduced the 'Me' and then reacts to it as an 'I'" (p.174). To be clear, the I and the me are not entities, they are points of reference in a continuing, emerging process. According to Mead:

> *The self involves a process that is going on, that takes on now one form and now another—a subject-object relationship which is dynamic, not static, a subject-object relationship which has a process behind it, one which can appear now in this phase, now in that. (p.13)*

In this process me is oneself visualized as an object in possible action or as having acted. I is oneself in the process of observing and responding to me. Said again, I is simply the experience of responding to objects. Me is simply experiencing oneself as an object, along with other objects. Significant symbols, the stuff of language, allow one to objectify and respond to oneself as others would do—specific others or others in general. That is, significant symbols, having the same meaning to oneself as to others, convey meaning as viewed by others. And, as one learns significant symbols, one learns to view oneself as others do. However, one can only see oneself as me, the object; one cannot see oneself as I, the subject. Yet, the response of I, once it occurs, immediately becomes observable as me. In the words of Mead, "The 'I' of this moment is present in the 'me' of the next moment" (p.174). As to an individual's response, Mead insists one does not control the response, rather one selects the stimulus (p.6n; p.128). This is a key distinction. The stimulus one selects is a suitable object, or objects—as objects are "collapsed acts." This includes viewing oneself—me—as an object, a collapsed act. And, one's response to a stimulus, contingent upon I's recognition, is an "emergent." That is, one's response is not preordained, but is fashioned in the interactive process—the interaction with oneself or with others.

To be sure, what Mead describes as the I—me—other interaction is a fleeting, evanescent process—one that is difficult to render in words. It is reminiscent of Peter Pan's difficulty—trying to capture his own shadow. By way of analogy, one might think of the process as similar to the dialectic. Me, oneself visualized or objectified in action, is "thesis." That is, it is oneself viewed in the factual, or putatively factual, ongoing course of events. Other is the borrowed perspectives of others (via significant symbols) with respect to possible options for me– alternative actions in a problematic situation. That is, other is "antithesis." One's internal dialogue of others offers different views on what me might to do. Finally, I is the restructuring of one's action as a result of taking the attitudes of others toward me's situation. Upon recognizing a solution by assuming various perspectives—that is, upon objectifying me in a successful course of action—I initiates this action. I is "synthesis," the emergent action. Synthesis is the reconstitution of action, allowing one's action to continue. As an illustration, consider the following personal narrative:

> » My ongoing action, e.g., driving an auto, washing dishes, taking a walk, is largely habitual.

> » In the course of my ongoing action, I select relevant objects, collapsed acts, and I respond.

> » At some point, the situation is problematic. There's no clear action; no clear identity of my action as an object, or set of objects—no collapsed act.

> » In response, I visualize myself, as me—from the perspectives of various others—engaging in various acts—acts which respond to a sequence of perceived or imagined objects.

> » Upon identifying a reconstituted act—the act as a reconstituted object, or set of objects—the response of I follows.

It is essential that one learn to see oneself as an object from a general, socially coherent perspective. According to Mead the mind, or personality, fully develops only when one is able to move from "play" to the "game"—two stages in the development of the self. In the play stage a child has learned to imitate a single role, the independent actions of one person. Mead says, "A child plays at being a mother, at being a teacher, at being a policeman; that is, it is taking different roles, as we say" (p.150). This is distinguished from the game, in which one mentally takes on a number of interacting roles. Mead continues, "The child who plays in a game must be ready to take the attitude of everyone else involved in that game, and… these different roles must have a definite relationship to each other" (p.151). Mead adds, "The fundamental difference between the game and play is that in the latter the child must have the attitude of all the others involved in that game" (p.153–154). For example, one can imagine participating in a game, any organized sport, and simultaneously imagine what one is doing and what all the other players are doing. One can also imaginatively move around the playing field, looking at the game from each player's perspective. This capacity is necessary for the complete self, the fully functioning personality, the effective player of the game. Again Mead states, "Only insofar as he takes the attitudes of the organized social group to which he belongs toward the organized, co-operative social activity or set of such activities in which that group is engaged, does he develop a complete self or possess the sort of complete self he has developed" (p.155). Such a broad, encompassing perspective is termed a "generalized other."

Mead proposes that "reflexivity," or mentally treating oneself as an object, is usually triggered by a problem that emerges and disrupts ongoing, largely habitual activity:

> *Mind, as constructive or reflective or problem-solving thinking, is the socially acquired means or mechanism or apparatus whereby the human individual solves the various problems of environmental adjustment which arise to confront him in the course of his experience, and which prevent his conduct from proceeding harmoniously on its way, until they have been dealt with (p.308).*

Action involving reflexive intelligence, in a process of problem solving, produces a continuing reconstruction of oneself, of social relations, indeed of society. Mead remarks, "And mind or thinking is also—as possessed by the individual members of society—the means or mechanism or apparatus whereby social reconstruction is affected or accomplished by these individuals" (p.308). Mead further states, "Social reconstruction and self or personality reconstruction are the two sides of a single process—the process of human social evolution" (p.309). In addition, as one takes reflexive action in the present, and thereby is constructing the future, one is also continually reconstructing the past. According to Mead, "The passing present, compounded of the past which is determined by the interpretation of the present and the future which comes to us as alternative possibilities, is what we have" (1972a, p.616). Elsewhere, Mead observes, "We are advancing constantly into a new universe; and, not only is the universe that we look forward into new, but, as we look back, we reinterpret the old universe. We have continually a different past" (1972b, p.291).

As one reconstructs action, using reflexive intelligence to resolve problems, one necessarily introduces new properties into social relations. That is, reflexive problem solving and the continuous reconstitution of social action introduce emergent properties. Said otherwise, as social objects are drawn into new contexts—different sets of purposeful relationships, different means and ends relations—new properties emerge. One may, for example, think of any number of inventions and scientific achievements that occurred simply because someone saw a problem in a different context, in terms of a different set of relationships. Modern industry has often adopted "skunk-works," deliberately marginal groups, to foster invention. In addition, one may say that creativity, innovation in society, comes disproportionately from socially marginal groups. Consider the role of African Americans and Jews in the arts. Simply put, emergence often occurs when, in the course of problem solving, objects, or parts thereof, are reconstituted by being placed in different contexts of meaning. Mead says, "However, I have defined emergence as the presence of things in two or more different systems, in such a fashion that its presence in a later system changes its character in the earlier system or systems to which it belongs" (1932, p.69). Accordingly, one may proffer that social action, whether external or internal, necessarily has unpredictable, emergent characteristics. As such, particular social actions cannot be mechanically attributed to preceding events.

> Within any society there is a continuing struggle over the dominant meaning of social relations.

Given the continuous construction and reconstruction of social life, any particular order in society is tenuous. As has been said by many sociologists in the symbolic interactionist tradition, society is a "negotiated order"—and a continuously renegotiated order (Strauss, 1963, passim). Stated otherwise, within any society there is a continuing struggle over the dominant meaning of social relations.

The negotiations concern such things as what is real, what is not real, what is important, what is not important, what is appropriate, what is not appropriate, and so on. The course of social action in any setting depends very significantly on the meaning attributed to it by participating individuals. Therefore, to understand human social action one must understand the meaning it has for such individuals. This recalls the dictum of W.I. Thomas, a prominent symbolic interactionist. Thomas declares, "If men define situations as real, they are real in their consequences." (1928, p. 572). One might add a corollary—insofar as circumstances are not defined as real, they are not likely to be real in consequences.

The centrality of meaning in human reflexive actions suggests such actions are "teleological." That is, mechanical causal explanations are not in order. Mead says this variously:

All acts, as such, are teleological. They move toward a result which is a success or a failure. (2011, p.21)

In our moral conduct we control our actions in considerable degree, i.e., in proportion as we are intelligent, by the ideas of results not yet attained. That is, our conduct is teleological. (1964, p.252)

Thus the first condition of consciousness is life... The second condition is that the living form in its teleological process can react, as a whole, purposively, to conditions of its own organism. (1932, p.69)

Mead's emphasis upon reflexive thought and action, purposefulness in action, a teleological orientation to action, means that analytically he places an emphasis upon "rationality" in social action. In this context rationality refers to an individual's conscious attention to the means and the ends of action. Central to reflexive conduct and to social dynamics there is a contention over various possible means and ends of social action. However, it does not mean that by some independent standard behavior is objectively rational. Mead makes comments such as the following about rationality in social action:

What we term 'reason' arises when one of the organisms takes into its own response the attitude of the other organisms involved. It is possible for the organism so to assume the attitudes of the group that are involved in its own act within this whole cooperative process. When it does so, it is what we term a 'rational being.' (1965a, p.334)

He belongs to a society of all rational beings, and the rationality that he identifies with himself involves a continual social interchange. (p.201)

Consistent with the pragmatist philosophical tradition, Mead views "truth" as that which works in practice. Placing this maxim in the context of reflexive problem solving he says:

Knowledge is a process in conduct that so organizes the field of action that delayed and inhibited responses may take place. The test of the success of the process of knowledge, that is, the

> *test of truth, is found in the discovery or construction of such objects as will mediate our conflicting and checked activities and allow conduct to proceed. (1932, p.68)*

Accordingly, truth, like society, is a continuously emerging process. It is ever changing. Reminiscent of Dewey's book, *The Quest for Certainty*, there simply is no certainty to be found in the study of social action and social relations. As a researcher one must anchor one's work in such presuppositions as, upon use, are reliable and sufficient to support inquiry. This is somewhat like house construction on the edge of rivers and lakes. In some locations the accumulated silt is so deep as to be apparently bottomless. The pilings to support houses cannot reach a solid foundation. So, the builders must rely upon a sufficient number of pilings, driven a sufficient depth into the soft ground, to provide sufficient support for a structure. Likewise, social science researchers must build upon presuppositions that have no certain basis, but are sufficiently well-founded to sustain their work and reliably contribute to solving problems.

As previously mentioned, Mead recognizes three early qualitative types of social action. Analytically, social action may be viewed as a mixture of the three types. He refers to the three qualitative types, or universals, as economic, as religious or neighborly, and as political or administrative. In addition, there is an underlying universal of language. Communication is essential to express the qualitative universals. Each of the three qualitative types is characterized by a fundamentally different attitude of other. That is, in each type of reflexive action a different kind of meaning prevails. Now, this centrality of meaning strongly suggests an "interpretative" approach to social analysis. The primary consideration in social research is what the social action means, or meant, to the participants. Thus sociologists following the lead of Mead usually favor qualitative methods such as participant observation, ethnography, historical narratives, case studies, and such. With these methods the researcher can become deeply immersed in the meaning of the action studied.

Mead defines "meaning" in terms of the "consequences" of social action. For the purposes of this essay meaning refers to the "presumed consequences" or "anticipated outcome" of an action. Thus, individuals who anticipate different outcomes of an action

> Meaning refers to the "presumed consequences" or "anticipated outcome" of an action.

necessarily attribute different meaning to the action. John Dewey, the eminent philosopher and close associate of Mead, explains meaning as follows:

> *Events have effects or consequences anyway; and since meaning is awareness of these consequences before they actually occur, reflective inquiry which converts an event into an object is the same thing as finding out a meaning which the event already possessed by imputation. (1929, p.324)*

In more esoteric language, Mead defines meaning in saying, "The response of one organism to the gesture of another in any given social act is the meaning of that gesture." (1965a, p.78). Of course, the response is a consequence of the gesture. It must also be said that meaning arises in the course of social action, including action with oneself, and does not inhere independently in things. And, speaking more broadly, meaning is a collective enterprise.

Associated with Mead's concept of meaning (as social consequence) is the idea, previously mentioned, that an object, any object, is a collapsed act. More loosely one might repeat a common phrase, "The test of pudding is in the eating." Mead phrases this idea variously: "The object is a collapsed act" (1972a, p.370), "the object of perception is the existent future of the act" (1932, p.190), and "objects are plans of action" (p.176). More simply, the meaning of a chair depends upon the intended outcome. Will it be used to sit upon? Will it be broken up and used as firewood? Will it be used as a weapon? Mead places this concept, that the object is a collapsed act, in the context of an individual's reflexive problem solving action. He says, "The immediate function of the appearance of the self in experience is that of analyzing the complex response, in the face of conflict, so that a new field of objects may appear together with a reconstituted act." (1972a, p.370). He also states, "The conflict, together with its inhibition, breaks up these objects, and it is not until new objects have arisen that intelligent conduct can proceed" (p.370). Said otherwise, individuals control their behavior by the selection of objects, objects which elicit particular acts. As noted earlier, Mead insists one controls behavior not by selection of the response, but by selection of the stimuli. Going a bit further, one might suggest that an event, a social event, may be seen as a string of objects, or a construction of objects, each of which is a collapsed act. And, one manages the event by rearranging and substituting social objects.

CHAPTER III

Max Weber

ollowing the discussion of Mead's ideas, a review of Max Weber's ideas is in order, ideas that are relevant to this essay. Later it will be apparent that in important respects their ideas are very similar. However, Weber's ideas are difficult to summarize, as he engaged in wide ranging intellectual activity. Living from April 21, 1864, to June 14, 1920, he was one of the greatest of German intellectuals. He was well known in his time, and remains well known, as a jurist, economist, historian, and one of the principal founders of sociology. As to sociology, Weber is primarily known for his large-scale, comparative studies of societies and institutions—from ancient times to the Twentieth Century. In addition, he did seminal work in establishing powerful sociological concepts and analytic methods. Yet, understanding and appreciation of Weber in the United States was hampered for a long time, as only a very limited portion of his work was translated into English. In his scholarly work Weber was particularly interested in understanding the origins of the distinctive characteristics of western societies. Bendix observes of Weber, "In his comparative studies he tried to lay the basis for establishing the mix of 'material' and 'ideal' factors accounting for the uniqueness of occidental history." (1977, p.xxiii). In addition, Weber was interested in the rise of rational social forces in societies, and particularly in the West. Thus, he was necessarily concerned with organizations and systems of authority.

In his sociological writings Weber objectifies social action in terms comparable to those cited earlier as the primary colors of social action. That is, he examines social processes in terms of the interplay of economic, social/cultural, and authority/political modes of action. According to Bendix (p.477), Weber believed, "All men are engaged in the pursuit of 'ideal and material interests.' In this pursuit they may be guided not only by considerations of utility and affinity but also by a belief in the existence of a legitimate order of authority." "Utility" refers, of course, to economic utility, and "affinity" refers to social or cultural affinity. "Authority" refers to "legitimate power," be it constituted by a state or another form of organization. And, the pursuit of legitimate power, or authority, is political action. In his numerous studies, Weber had a particular concern with the reciprocal influence of religious and economic action. Bendix notes, "We saw that Weber analyzed the influence of religious ideas on economic behavior as well as the influence that the interest in material gains and social honor can have upon the development of religious ideas." (p.286). Weber's most widely read book, *The Protestant Ethic and the Spirit of Capitalism*, is a case in point—the engagement of religious and economic interests. Much of Weber's concern with authority and political action was expressed in comparative studies of governance in states and other organizations.

In the present essay various terms will be used, depending upon context, in referring to action in each realm: economic, social, and political. However, always these translate into orientations to action that Weber termed "material interests," "ideal interests," and interests in "legitimate power." Typically, this essay will refer to economic, social or cultural, and authority or political orientations to action. Thus, although Weber discussed many types of social action, this essay will focus on the types of action, the principal action orientations (i.e., meanings), that inform collective action and the structure of Weber's analytic concepts. In a thorough assessment of Weber's work, Kalberg asserts three types of "rationality"—"practical," "substantive," and "formal"—"directly orders action into patterns" (1980, p.1160-1161). These accord with the economic, social or cultural and authority or political dimensions in this essay. Weber's distinction of three modes of collective action appears repeatedly in his conceptual schemes. Bendix states, "Weber's definitions of sociological concepts (in theory) were an effort to 'decompose' three overlapping dimensions of social life—authority, material interest, and value orientation—into their separate parts." (p.286). For example, Weber notes there are three orders of stratification in society: "economic," "status," and "legal" (authority). Within these orders, individuals and groups are distributed by "economic classes," "status groups," and "parties." Further, these groupings exemplify the three bases of collective action within society—solidarity due to shared economic interests, solidarity due to shared ideas, and solidarity based on allegiance to authority. However, Bendix implies a conceptual distinction (to be examined later) between solidarity formed by ideas or interests, on one hand, and by authority, on the other:

> *Though Weber nowhere discussed its significance for his work, it may be suggested that for him the conditions of solidarity on the basis of ideas or interests and the moral order of authority on the basis of a belief in legitimacy were the two perspectives through which a comprehensive view of society could be obtained. (p.287-288)*

In any society it is likely one order will be dominant, thus Weber states there are class (economic) or status (social/cultural) societies. That is, "Depending upon the prevailing mode of stratification, we shall speak of a 'status society' or a 'class society.'" (1978, p.306). Had Weber lived long enough to witness Nazi, Fascist, Stalinist, and Maoist regimes, he probably would have added "political" or "party" societies. In such totalitarian societies, the political party and political/authority dimension dominate the class and status orders. Weber uses numerous other conceptual distinctions based on the three dimensions of social action. Swedberg notes, for example, "There are economic, religious and political associations or organizations within society." (2005 p. 187). Also, Weber recognized three types of legitimate power, or authority, in social relations. Authority may be justified on "rational grounds," "traditional grounds," or "charismatic grounds." In addition, Weber states that parties retain the support of party followers by means of "sinecures," "power," and "honor." (1946, p.194). These, of course, reflect the economic, political, and social dimensions respectively. Further, Weber distinguishes three types of political parties: "patronage parties," "ideological parties," and "charismatic parties." (Swedberg, 2005, p.194). Again, these distinctions reflect the economic, social, and political dimensions. Patronage parties, of course, principally enlist support with economic benefits. In contrast, the social, or cultural, dimension is the realm of beliefs, values, and norms. Thus ideological parties principally enlist support in the social dimension. As to "charisma," later this essay will suggest it is the purest,

> "Charisma"… is the purest, least adulterated orientation to authority… in its ideal, perfected form, charisma stands uncompromised by material or ideal interests.

least adulterated orientation to authority. That is, in its ideal, perfected form, charisma stands uncompromised by material or ideal interests.In sum, conceptual distinctions reflecting the three dimension of action—economic, social/cultural, and authority/political— appear throughout Weber's work.

Weber was strongly opposed to what is generally termed "positivism" in the social sciences. He rejected the idea that social science concepts and methods must imitate those of the natural sciences. In this respect, he stood opposed to Durkheim, another founder of sociology, and to many other sociologists in the Twentieth Century. According to Heckman, Weber rejected both positivism and subjectivism and countered with his own methodology (1983, p.27). Neither objective nor subjective aspects of social behavior are to be given primacy in sociology. Rather social behavior consists of objective actions "constituted by the meaning bestowal of social actors." (p.29). Also in opposition to positivism, Weber rejected the pursuit of causal laws in the social sciences. Heckman says:

> *Thus, the discovery of a universal law, however significant in some scientific investigations, is not significant in the social sciences… Hence he concludes that universal laws are simply not relevant to the concerns of the social sciences and must be rejected as the proper methodological tools of the social sciences. (p.35-36)*

Pascale similarly reports:

> *According to Weber, laws are only conceptual aids for understanding reality. Weber (1978) argued that knowledge of cultural process is possible only by understanding the meanings that the specific and shared reality holds for those involved. (2010, p.77)*

Weber employed the term *verstehen*—one aims to understand action in terms of its meaning to participants. The construction of an "interpretative understanding" of social events is the prime objective of sociological inquiry. In Weber's own words:

> The construction of an "interpretative understanding" of social events is the prime objective of sociological inquiry.

> *Sociology (in the sense in which this highly ambiguous word is used here) is a science concerning itself with the interpretative understanding of social action and thereby with a causal explanation of its course and consequences. We shall speak of 'action' insofar as the acting individual attaches a subjective meaning to his behavior—be it overt or covert, commission or acquiesce. (1978, p.4)*

Appleroth says, "In casting 'interpretative understanding,' or *Verstehen*, as the principal objective, Weber's vision of sociology offers a distinctive counter to those who sought to base the young discipline on the effort to uncover universal laws applicable to all societies." (2008, p.143).

With respect to causality in social action, Weber embraced a position that is essentially teleological. In reference to Weber, the Stanford Encyclopedia of Philosophy states, "A teleological contextualization of an action in the means—end nexus is indeed a precondition for a causal explanation that can be objectively ascertained." (2007, p.11–12). Thus, any sensible use of the idea of causality in social action must refer to the purposiveness, or intended outcome of such action. Swedberg comments in reference to Weber:

> *The social scientist has to proceed in a somewhat similar fashion to legal reasoning: inquire into the motives of the actor and then try to establish to what extent his or her behavior can reasonably be said to have the effect that is at issue. (2005, p.30)*

Weber termed this a "correct causal interpretation":

> *A correct causal interpretation of typical action means that the process which is claimed to be typical is shown to be both adequately grasped on the level of meaning and at the same time the interpretation is to some degree causally adequate ... a probability that action in fact normally takes the course which has been held to be meaningful. (1978, p.12)*

To pursue his objective of interpretive understanding, Weber constructed and used qualitative types in the comparative analyses of social action. These qualitative types, called "ideal types," do not exist in reality (Heckman, 1983, passim). They are conceptual exaggerations of real phenomena that are used for purposes of comparison and analysis of real phenomena. Ideal type concepts are used to identify and pull apart, to sort out, the various threads of meaningful action in complex social action. Examples of ideal type concepts are abundant in everyday life. Vast numbers of people have observed on television Olympic ice skating, diving, and gymnastics competition. Each sport has one or more conceptions of an ideal, or perfect, performance. Although some competitors may score at or near the maximum points, presumably every performance has some fault, some error. But, each ideal serves as a gauge, a standard, for assessing that type of action. Weber originated, or perfected, many ideal type constructs widely used today as sociological concepts. The examples previously mentioned are his types of authority, types of societies, types of stratification, and so on.

Weber saw recurrent patterns of action, or structural arrangements in society, not as based upon a positivistic causality, but upon "elective affinity." This means that linkages of social components are principally due to a compatibility of meaning—meaning as understood by the social actors.

According to Stark, Weber saw the relationship of Protestantism and capitalism not as causal, but that groups of men "made the religious philosophy and moral code their own because they found it convenient, attractive, sympathetic, sinnverswandt [meaningful]," (p.258). Bendix clarifies Weber's use of elective affinity by example:

> "Elective affinity" ... means that linkages of social components are principally due to a compatibility of meaning—meaning as understood by the social actors.

> *The group providing religious leadership in a civilization will tend to formulate the prevailing concept of the deity in a manner that 'fits in' with their basic political experience…*

> *For example, warriors usually develop a strong identification with military strength; hence they will tend to reject the idea of religious humility, but they also will become fighters for the faith and adhere to religious ideas that are consonant with the military virtues. (p.270-271)*

Weber states the following in opposing the idea of causal laws of social development:

The mental construct of a cultural stage merely means, analytically speaking, that the individual phenomena of which it is composed are "adequate" to one another, that they have — as we could say — a certain measure of inner "affinity," but not that they are related in any determinate way. (1978, p.xLIV)

With regard to the structure of social action, Weber viewed struggle within a society over its defining characteristics as omnipresent, as inevitable. This is a struggle of economic classes and their material interests, as envisioned by Marx. However, added to this is the struggle of status groups and their ideal interests. Status groups generally seek to privilege, and perhaps impose, their beliefs, values, and norms. In addition, parties struggle over the disposition and exercise of authority. Later, the struggle over authority will be discussed as a struggle over making "collective decisions." Given a system of authority, whether in a state or another organization, one must assume there is always some contention over its allocation and use. In any case, those in each type of grouping—class, status group, or party—tend to seek their own form of dominance. Altogether, the struggle in an organization is a mix of action by such groupings. Said otherwise, it is a struggle over the predominant meaning of social action. Furthermore, the outcome of such contention is always in some respects unpredictable.

Weber emphasized the importance of emergent properties in social action. This is particularly true with regard to the effect of charismatic authority. Inasmuch as charismatic leadership tends to ignore, or outright violate, traditional practices and established rules, it is likely the bearer of unanticipated change, innovation, path breaking solutions to problems, etc. Gerth and Mills make the following comment:

Just as for George H. Mead the 'I' is ordinarily in tension with social roles derived from the expectations of others, so for Weber the potentially charismatic quality of man stands in tension with the external demands of institutional life. (1946, p.73)

Charismatic action is an ever present possibility in social action. Edward Shils suggested that charismatic action is far more common than most social theorists have allowed (1965, p.199–213). It should not be seen as existing only in very exceptional and extreme circumstances. It is deeply woven into the fabric of social relations. For example, one may recall that even the head of a bureaucracy is always, to some extent, a non-bureaucratic head (Parsons, 1947, p.335). With this consideration of charisma, the brief exposition of Weber's ideas concludes. There are many other important aspects of Weber's work that could be mentioned, but the aforesaid are perhaps most relevant to this essay.

At this point it is apparent there are a number of similarities in the thinking of Weber and Mead:

» To understand social behavior one must know what it means to participants.

» Inquiry seeks to establish interpretative/reflexive understanding of action.

» There are three principal orientations/attitudes of individuals in social action: economic, cultural/social, and authority/political.

» All social action is action of individuals, i.e., methodological individualism. Sociological concepts may be viewed as real, and be real in their consequences, but they are abstractions from individual action.

» The social action of individuals is teleological.

» There is a similitude of individual reflexivity and organizational rationality.

» Emergent properties are characteristic of social relations.

» The social world is continuously reconstructed through purposeful action.

» There is an endless struggle over social construction and reconstruction.

» Positivistic assumptions and concepts are categorically rejected.

» The focus on meaning requires qualitative research methodology.

As the essay proceeds additional similarities will appear, including those of Mead and Weber's central concepts, and these similarities will be reviewed in the final chapter. At this point, discussion turns to the consideration of complex organization, or rather "organized action" (Weber, 1978, p.lxxxiii; p.48). The intent is to increase reflexive/rational understanding of the forces that shape organized action.

> The intent is to increase reflexive/rational understanding of the forces that shape organized action.

CHAPTER IV

Emergence

Surprisingly, studies of organizations don't always clearly specify what they mean by an organization. Of course, individuals generally know an organization when they see one. In one's local community are churches, schools, businesses, civic associations, local government agencies, and so forth. On a larger scale there are such examples as state or national governments, national public interest organizations, branches of the military, and national or multinational corporations. Some organizations employ thousands of individuals. Modern society, in fact, is dominated by large organizations; they are ubiquitous. But, sociologically and analytically speaking, what is an organization? More particularly, from a symbolic interactionist perspective what is organized action?

One may start with the idea that organizations are a form of human "social group." That is, they appear to have all the attributes of social groups. However, society includes many social groups that generally are not organizations. For example, a family, a peer group, or a study group—none of these is likely to be an organization. One may say society itself is a large group, whereas the state is an organization. But, what then is a group? A simple collection, or "aggregate," of individuals is for the purposes of this essay not a social group. For example, a theatre audience, the patients in a waiting room, a check-out line in a grocery store, the patrons at a restaurant, or the clients at a government agency—none of these is a social group in the present meaning of the term. An aggregate is just a number of individuals. They are a collection simply by virtue of some similarity of circumstance, experience, or other social characteristic. Unlike a social group, as the term is used here, the whole of an aggregate is not more than the sum of its constituent parts. Said otherwise, with an aggregate there's nothing distinctive about the gathering that an outsider, experienced in the broader culture of such persons, would not understand. There are no special phrases, secrets, insider jokes, catch words, and such. Also, there are no distinctive patterns of action, habits, routines, that are peculiar to the aggregate. The mere assemblage of persons as an aggregate does not immediately have, within itself, the multiplier or generative effect—being more than the sum of its parts—that may come with extended interaction.

A social group has emergent properties not possessed by simple aggregates. At this point, two emergent qualities are of particular importance. They are group "structure" and group "culture." The concept that social groups, including organizations, have structure and culture is widely recognized. For example, in a sociology textbook Eitzen and Zinn state, "A group is a collection of people who, because of sustained interaction, have evolved a common structure and culture" (2001, p.28). In a classic book on organizations, Blau and Scott agree, "These two dimensions of social organization—the networks of social relations and the shared orientations—are often referred to as the social structure and the culture, respectively" (1962, p.4). Accordingly, one may stipulate that any social group has a distinctive structure and culture. Eitzen and Zinn (2005, p.28), and Blau and Scott (p.2) further agree that— within groups or organizations— structure and culture serve to constrain or guide the actions of individuals. As used herein, the term culture refers to the ideational aspects of group and organizational action. More specifically it refers to beliefs, values, and norms. As used herein, the term structure refers to established, overt patterns of action or interaction. These are such things as a division of labor, daily routines, patterns of communication, and such. So, in the present discussion what distinguishes a group from a mere aggregate of individuals is a distinctive and enduring set of shared ideas and a distinctive and enduing set of patterned, overt activities.

Structure and culture in a social group express the duality that is characteristic of all human social action. However, as said, in a particular social group it is a distinctive duality. A number of theorists have described human social groups in terms of a duality of objective and subjective characteristics. Kingsley Davis declares that human society has "not merely the objective set of relationships between members, but the subjective norms as well." (1957, p.52–53). He describes it as a "double reality," with the "factual order" embodying "what is" and the "normative order" embodying "what ought to be." This duality is of special concern to those theorists, such as Mead and Weber, who emphasize meaning and seek an interpretative understanding of social action. As mentioned previously, in contrast to some positivist theorists Weber's idea of social action includes a balanced consideration of objective behavior and subjective intent. According to Susan Heckman, "Weber always identifies an action by specifying its subjective meaning and by identifying the particular course of action that is linked to this meaning." (1983, p.51). With respect to Mead, he explicitly recognizes the duality of social action in his explanation of social relations and the development of the individual personality. These depend upon significant symbols, which in interpersonal social interactions are overt actions and convey the subjective meaning of action. Indeed, the two words, "symbolic interaction," as coined by Herbert Blumer, convey the duality of social action. Blumer observes that such a duality accords with common sense and "might be expressed in the statement that an individual acts toward objects in terms of what they mean to him." (1986, p.118). So, group action has two dimensions that are distinctive: a factual, objective, structural dimension, and a normative, largely subjective, cultural dimension.

An aggregate of individuals who continuously interact are likely to develop group characteristics. Again, Eitzen and Zinn note that structure and culture "emerge through enduring social interaction." (2001, p.49). In time, interaction among members of an aggregate will demonstrate somewhat distinctive ideas—beliefs, values, norms—and somewhat distinctive patterns of action. Accordingly, one may say that a group is more than the sum, the aggregate, of its constituent individuals. This is expressed as follows by Blau and Scott:

> *In short, a network of social relations transforms an aggregate of individuals into a group (or an aggregate of groups into a larger social structure), and the group is more than the sum of the individuals composing it since the structure of social relations is an emergent element that influences the conduct of individuals. (1962, p.3)*

One may think of several analogies: a cake is more than the sum of ingredients in its recipe, a song is more than a sum of musical notes, and a painting is more than a mix of colors. In each case, the constituent elements are place in an objectively and subjectively meaningful relationship. Again, such distinctions are viewed as qualitative. Their relationship to social action rests upon an interpretation of meaning and a corresponding assessment of qualitative difference.

As said, group structure and culture are emergent qualities of social groups. They arise from extended interaction within such groups. Further, one may expect extended interaction within a social group to continuously produce additional emergents. However, these additional qualities will be particular manifestations of structure and culture. The question as to distinguishing additional emergents ultimately is a matter of what group participants see as meaningful—inasmuch as qualities are attributes by which things are judged to be similar or different. For the purposes here it may be appropriate to recognize some of these additional qualities. That is, they may prove to be useful distinctions for interpretive understanding of action in a social group. One such quality is a shared belief among group members of their common "identity." That is, a common understanding of whom they are as a group. Another such quality is a preference and a practice of "exclusivity." A third possibility is secret "rituals" and "ceremonies" which convey special meanings. A fourth possibility is an explicit "code" of appropriate, or honorable, behavior. In addition, many other comparable developments are possible.

One of the most significant emergents from group action is what is commonly referred to as "community." Community, as a term, may be said to subsume many of the previously mentioned emergents, as well as others. According to Weber, communal action exists when people feel they belong together (1946, p.183). In Mead's terms, community is based on a group's shared understandings about such things as what to believe, what has value, and how one should act in various circumstances (1965A, p.264–265). Blumer brings these views together in the following statement:

> *I think we should make clear that when we speak of the "voice of the community," we mean attitudes, beliefs, ways of behaving that are shared and approved by members of the community and especially that the individual who listens to that voice is also a member of that community, his voice is included, his attitudes, etc. are included. (2004, p.114)*

Consistent with these thoughts, Anthony Cohen asserts that community is principally based on a social group's shared culture (1985, passim). This point will be revisited in some detail later in this essay.

Structure and culture are not fanciful, non-empirical attributes of group action. One can see group structure, patterns of behavior. Coming upon a collection of individuals and patiently observing them, one can fairly reliably determine if they are a group, several groups, or not a group at all. One can observe, for example, the sharing of tasks and of the resources necessary to perform the tasks. One can observe the sharing of leisure, of consumables, of personal space, and so forth. One can also observe evidence of a common culture—written or spoken words, gestures, etc. Given time, one will undoubtedly come to understand some of the group's unique communications.

The foregoing discussion has considered group action, as contrasted to aggregate action. Group action involves distinctive structure and culture. In addition, one may distinguish other emergent qualities. What, then, is organized action, which has been identified as a form of social group action? With respect to organized action, or action pertaining to organizations, one may posit specific emergent qualities. In particular, one may suggest an additional primary quality to those of structure and culture. At the same time, one must remain clear that these are abstractions, or generalizations, constructed for analytic purposes. The interest here is collective action—specifically aggregate action, group action, and organized action. In the context of this essay, these forms of action altogether constitute social structure.

> Aggregate action, group action, and organized action. In the context of this essay, these forms of action altogether constitute social structure.

Unlike much of organizational theory this essay will not be concerned with aggregate, group, or organizational "boundaries" and whether certain individuals and their actions are in or out. As a matter of reference, there are many things that exist but do not have definite, identifiable boundaries. One might mention a cloud or a fog, a wind, tornado, or hurricane, a celestial galaxy, a crowd, a social movement, a consumer market. Here the concern is not with delineating an entity or its boundaries, but with understanding a collective process. More broadly, this essay is not concerned with claims about determinate relations among objective facts. It outlines an approach—an approach based on Mead and Weber—to interpretative understanding of social action, large or small, organized or unorganized.

CHAPTER V.

Reflexivity

The term organized action refers to the type of social action characteristic of government agencies, business organizations, membership associations, religious congregations, universities or colleges, community hospitals, etc. This kind of social action is often called "complex" or "formal" organization. Presumably agreement can be reached that such an organization is a form of social group. And, inasmuch as an organization is some form of group, it necessarily has the two primary dimensions previously attributed to group action. A particular organization will have distinctive patterns of action and distinctive cultural elements. It will have, for example, some structure of tasks and some set of norms. What, then, distinguishes organizations from other social groups that are not organizations? After Weber, the foremost scholar of organizations, one may say that organized group action has a third dimension—some form of administration, an explicit delegation of authority by group participants. According to Weber, a number of characteristics are associated with organized action, such as "rules" and a "defined membership," but the essential characteristic is an administration, an explicit arrangement of authority. Weber states, "Whether or not an organization exists is entirely a matter of the presence of a person in authority, with or without an administrative staff." (1978, p.49). Paraphrasing Weber, an organization may be said to exist insofar as a group has an effective arrangement for the delegation of authority.

In conventional terms, the authority arrangement within an organization is expected to do such things as coordinate group activities, promulgate and enforce rules, set objectives and policies, allocate tasks, supervise performance, problem solve, and the like. In contrast to a simple group, then, one may say that an organization has not two but three primary dimensions of meaningful action. Organized action formalizes

> An organization may be said to exist insofar as a group has an effective arrangement for the delegation of authority.

the fact that any purposive course of action includes not only objective and subjective aspects, but necessarily the subordination of some comprised actions to others. In the words of Mead, "The later stages of the act are present in the early stages-not simply in the sense that they are all ready to go off, but in the sense that they serve to control the process itself," (1965A, p.11). That is, consummatory action tends to control the foregoing action.

The recognition of what has been called structure, culture, and administration—or an authority arrangement—as dimensions of organized action is consistent with the views of other organizational scholars. For example, in somewhat different terms, and within a systems framework, Katz and Kahn cite three essentials of an organization—which may be placed in the structural, cultural, and authority dimensions:

> *The forces which maintain the role system are the task demands, the shared values, and the observance of rules. Organizations develop out of more primitive groupings in which these first two forces many have been dominant, but they grow by formal elaboration of the third factor of rule enforcement. (1965, p.455)*

Shortly rules and rule enforcement will be clarified. The main point is that adding some form of explicit authority relations to a group produces organized action. It moves one from group action to organized group action. Thus, within the context of this essay an organization has a structure of practices for accomplishing

> Any purposive course of action includes not only objective and subjective aspects, but necessarily the subordination of some comprised actions to others.

collective tasks, embodies certain beliefs, values, and norms in a culture, and has an arrangement or system of authority. Furthermore what is true of the organization as a whole is true for each subpart of the organization. Each division, department, work group, or individual role in organized action has a particular structure of behavior, particular elements of organizational culture, and a particular delegation of authority. For example, a department is but organized action subsumed within larger organized action. As mentioned previously, organized action is an emergent quality. One may say an organization exists to the extent, and in the manner, that a social group exhibits this quality—that individual action is subject to organizational authority. Weber points out the transition from "consensual action," action principally "in accord with norms," to an "association" form of action, that is rational, organizational action, is fluid—"its extent and meaning may vary greatly." (1978, p.1379). Mead would certainly agree that organized action varies in the extent and manner it is rational—or collectively reflexive.

Along with administration Weber makes reference to rules and rule enforcement as characteristic of organized action. The question arises, "What are rules?" Rules according to several authors may be viewed as "preformed decisions." That is, they are decisions made in advance, or perhaps timeless decisions. For example, in referring to legal rules which support markets and allow or foster individual choice, Friedman calls such rules "preformed decisions." (1975, p.24). Similarly, Kaufman refers to what might ordinarily be called rules, or perhaps policy, in the U.S. Forest Service as "preformed decisions." (2006, passim). He cites "advance decisions announced by Forest Service leaders in the form of authorizations, directions, prohibitions, clearances, settlements of disputes" and other such matters. Thus, within this essay a rule will be defined as a decision with general and enduring properties. It is assumed that defining rules in this manner accords with Mead's concept of individual reflexivity and Weber's concept of organizational rationality.

The essential feature of authority, or administrative action, is explicit decision making on behalf of a social group. That is, whatever administrative action or exercise of authority takes place in an organization, the common thread is the making of collective decisions. Accordingly, one may say that adding some form of authority, that is, designating someone to make decisions and act on behalf of the entire group, produces organized group action. If this becomes established as a pattern, the group is to that extent engaging in organized activity. It is arbitrary, or simply a matter of analytic convenience, at what point one calls organized action an organization. This concept of administration, or authority, as an arrangement of collective decision making is similar to the viewpoint of Herbert Simon. Simon states, "It should be noted that the administrative processes are decisional processes." (1957, p.8). He further elaborates, "The anatomy of the organization is to be found in the distribution and allocation of decision-making functions." (p.220). Thus, one may accurately describe an organization in terms of what decisions each member makes and the influences upon these decisions. This view is echoed by other organizational theorists. According to Katz and Kahn, "The authority structure essentially describes the way in which the management system is organized with respect to the sources of decision making and its implementation." (1965, p.44).

The idea that organizational authority is essentially a matter of making decisions was succinctly stated by President George W. Bush (2006). When queried about his appointment of Donald Rumsfeld as Secretary of Defense he said, "I'm the decider and I decide what's best." Within this essay organizational authority is principally the architecture of collective decision making.

Various qualitative types of decision making are differentially placed throughout an organization. The reallocation of authority, or decision making on behalf on an entire group, is generally done by explicit delegation. Very likely the delegation is done in the manner of a rational scheme, with particular ends in mind. Furthermore, the reallocation of decision making throughout an organization is reinforced by other aspects of organizational structure and culture.

> Organizational authority is principally the architecture of collective decision making.

A necessary feature of a system of authority—particularly as rational action is emphasized—is the subordination of some actions, hence some actors, to others. Accordingly, organized action differs from simple group action in that all members must explicitly cede some personal control to the arrangement for collective decision making, or organizational authority. Upon entering an organization an individual surrenders decision making over some aspects of his or her behavior. This is palpable in some instances, for example the military. Doing so facilitates the development of complex and purposefully adaptive group behavior. An organization must restrain individual discretion—self directed, reflexive action—to some extent if it is to achieve collective purpose. Members cannot be allowed to do just anything they choose to do. Some organizations enforce rules (i.e., preformed decisions) with respect to dress code, the making of public comments, personal hygiene, and so forth. But the discretion of most individuals must be limited with respect to altering the basic means and ends of an organization. Thus, when an individual becomes a regular participant in an organization, some of what was formerly his or her personal behavior now becomes the organization's behavior. Simon affirms this point, "The organization, then, takes from the individual some of his decisional autonomy, and substitutes for it an organizational decision-making process." (1957, p.8). That is, very largely an organization is a social machine (Weber, 1978, p.943; p.1156).

Although individual decision making is curtailed in an organization, decision making is also conferred upon all individuals. The organization delegates some decision making—on behalf of the entire organization—to every individual. At least it does so in principle. However low an individual may be in an organization, he or she necessarily exercises some discretion in the performance of organizational actions. An individual may not be allowed to decide when to come to work, or when to go to lunch, but may decide which packages are given priority in organizational mailings. The delegation of decision making on behalf of the organization exists throughout the organization. According to Simon:

> *It follows that authority, in the sense here defined, can operate "upward" and "sidewise" as well as "downward" in the organization. If an executive delegates to his secretary a decision about file cabinets and accepts her recommendation without reexamination of its merits, he is accepting her authority. (1957, p.12)*

As a practical matter in organized action, as it other action, what individuals are expected to know, or do, cannot be limitless. The decision making of individuals in an organization expresses a limited, or "bounded," rationality, and the choices made are "satisficing," or "good enough," not superlative. This idea has been discussed extensively by Herbert Simon. One may note parenthetically that it succinctly states the pragmatic idea of truth, i.e., truth is what works. Speaking of organizational problem solving, Simon states:

> *In actual practice, no one tries to find an optimal solution for the whole problem. Instead, various particular decisions are made by particular units of the organization. In making their decisions, the specialized units find a "satisfactory" solution for one or more subproblems, where some of the effects of*

> *the solution on other parts of the system are incorporated, as constraints, in the definition of "satisfactory." (1997, p.160)*

Commenting upon Simon's assertion, Perrow says:

> *The importance of this assumption about human beings is that it gives to organizational variables (division of labor, communication system, etc.) the predominant control over individual behavior… It calls for simplifying models of individual behavior in order to capture the complexities of organizational behavior. (1986, p.122)*

Said otherwise, when one enters an organization, one enters a context of delimited individual reflexive action. However, this is rationality that is deliberately limited with a larger set of means and ends in mind.

The emergence of authority, or administratively oriented action, makes a significant qualitative change in group action. To borrow Davis's terms, if the task structure (or factual) dimension refers to what "is," and the cultural (or normative) dimension refers to what "ought to be," then one may say the administrative (or authority) dimension refers to what "is becoming." This is illustrated in organized group action by such decision making as planning, problem solving, innovation, and other forward looking, leadership or management activities. The greater an individual's span of authority in an organization, generally speaking, the more forward looking his or her tasks. Thus, an authority system, or administration, provides a vehicle, but not the only possible vehicle, for introducing or emphasizing rational forms of collective action in a social group. This is not to say that organized action is rational by some objective standard, merely that there is some underlying rational orientation to action. The action has some rational meaning. Nor is it to say that the rational orientation is highly conscious among organizational participants. It is more likely to be conscious among those with greater authority in the organization.

Organizations, by offering the possibility of rational action, increase the collective power of a social group. By what one may call "collective reflexive action," organizational means are more effectively related to organizational ends. Organizations increase power by increasing the coherency, the logical consistency of group action. This confers the possibility of more efficient and more effective collective action. Hence, it facilitates the development of complex and purposefully adaptive group behavior. It also offers the possibility of seemingly unlimited linking, or compounding, of more simple forms of organized action. It was said that organizational rationality requires interpersonal dominance. This means the subordination of some means to other means, and some individuals or groups to others. Such subordination includes the likelihood, but not the necessity, of a hierarchy.

Simon observes that within an organization there are a variety of perspectives on what constitutes a rational orientation to action (1957, p.76–77). He suggests, "Perhaps the only way to avoid, or clarify, these complexities is to use the term 'rational' in conjunction with appropriate adverbs." In response to Simon one must reply that rationality of organized action is subject to a constant struggle within organizations. Herein the focus will be on forming an interpretative understanding of the struggle, its various participants, and their contributions to the ensuing course of action—past, present, or prospective. However, discussion of the struggle over establishing organizational means and ends brings to the fore the topic of organizational politics. Recalling an earlier statement, politics is the struggle over authority. One must understand from the outset that developing an organization and thereby exercising leadership is a political process. That is, it deals with how to motivate individuals in a common pursuit. It deals with how to control, how to dominate individuals. Organizations are, at core, political constructs. Recognizing the political character of administration, of delegated decision making, one may see an organization as ongoing group action—but it is an evolving, constantly changing, adapting, unsettled group action.

The development of organized group action may be illustrated by an imaginary progression from informal, sand-lot baseball to organized, team competition. At the informal level individuals may arrive at their leisure and join the group's customary routine of play, perhaps fitting in wherever there is an opening. The makeup of the game is adjusted to the number of players and the available playing field. In the organized activity of a team, however, decision making is delegated to one or more individuals with regard to opponents, time and place of play, who will play which position, bating rotation, and so on. The team manager, not the player, may decide whether the player swings hard at a ball, tries to draw a "base on balls," runs to "steal a base," or makes a "bunt." Team organization may progress to the point of sponsor-provided uniforms and equipment, recruitment of skilled players, monetary compensation, coaching staff to direct player actions on the field, and so forth. It may become a continuous, full-time activity, an organized league, with record keeping, formal rules, standardization of equipment, and so forth—ultimately a nascent form of Weber's model of "bureaucracy," or highly rationalized group action

(1978, p.956–958). Thus formal, collective decision making somewhat displaces informal, individual decision making.

Mead speaks of the reflexive process in which an individual person reconstitutes problematic or interrupted action by symbolically viewing the self from the point of view of others. It can be added that the rational administrative action of an organization is an analog to the reflexive intelligence of an individual as described by Mead. This should come as no surprise, as Mead repeatedly insists the individual's reflexive action is derived from rational social action. In many ways, organized action is the attempt to get a group of persons to act as one—one reflexive individual. Reflexivity, objectifying oneself in action, portraying various possible actions, is made explicit in an organization. This is illustrated by such things as organizational charts, job descriptions, training programs, etc. Indeed, it can often be the function of paid consultants to come into an organization and perform this reflexive function. In both cases, individual and organizational, a part of the action doubles back on the remainder—as a monitoring, decisional process. The individual monitors and adjusts his or her own action as needed or desired. The executive monitors and adjusts his or her organization's action as needed or desired. In what one may call administration, management, or perhaps leadership tasks, a subset of organizational action is directed back on the group's actions, as a whole or in part. The relationship of management—the decision making body—to the remainder of the organization is reflexive. In this respect it corresponds to the reflexivity of an individual. In a social group one may distinguish a structure, or objective component of action. One may also distinguish a culture, or subjective component of action. Additionally, in organized action one may distinguish a reflexive component of authority, of administration, of accompanying political action. And, just as individual action varies in the extent to which it is reflexive, group action also varies in the extent to which it is reflexive—or rationally ordered.

In organizations, as with individuals, the reflexive process is emphasized in problematic situations. Both involve what one may call "a process of analysis." That is, one conceptually breaks problematic action into parts, rearranges, alters, substitutes the means of action, and perhaps rearranges, alters, substitutes the ends of action, as well. Decisions, whether by the individual or an organization, are made by symbolically assembling and testing possible courses of action. Inasmuch as objects are collapsed acts, one may think of reflexive decision making as a process of identifying, selecting, rearranging a set of conceptual objects. Herbert Blumer noted the similarity of rational action in an organization with the reflexive action of an individual:

The same sort of picture exists in the case of the social action of a collectivity, such as a business corporation, a labor union, an army, a church, a boy's gang, or a nation. The difference is that the collectivity has a directing group or individual who is empowered to assess the operating situation, to note different things that have to be dealt with, and to map out a line of action. The self-interaction of a collectivity is in the same position as the individual in having to cope with a situation, in having to interpret and analyze the situation, and in having to construct a line of action. (1986, pp. 55-56)

As previously stated, reflexivity in social action is the ability to use symbols to objectify oneself and others, to assemble hypothetical courses of action, and to assess the probable outcomes of action. The fact that individual intelligent problem solving is an analogue, or parallels, organizational problem solving is precisely how it is that individuals can consciously work together in an organized manner to solve problems. It also indicates why this essay is concerned with the sociology of organized action. It is a useful context to explore the similarities in Mead and Weber's thinking. Individual reflexive action was a central focus for Mead, as were organizations and rationality in societies a central focus for Weber.

CHAPTER VI.

Meaning

The foregoing discussion has identified three dimensions of organized action. They have generally been referred to as structure, culture, and authority. Said otherwise, there are established patterns of action, shared ideas, and an accepted form of coordination or control. More particularly, within organized action structure is principally the distribution of (objective) "tasks and exchange relations." Culture is principally the distribution of (subjective) "beliefs, values, and norms." Authority is principally the distribution of (reflexive) "collective decision making"—decision making on behalf of the organized group. It is important to remember that these three dimensions overlap. Or, as Daniel Bell (Harvard lectures) often said, they are "interlarded." Thus, any organizational participant is simultaneously a participant in an organization's pattern of activities, or structure, a participant in the organization's culture, and a participant in the organization's authority arrangement. Said otherwise, any organizational action simultaneously relates to the organizational structure, culture, and authority system. A valid organizational action is presumed to carry out, in whole or in part, an organizational task, express or share organizational ideas, and comply with the dictates of authority. Again, these are analytical distinctions, inasmuch as behavior is a whole. These and other concepts are put forward for the interpretative understanding of collective actions. They are sensitizing concepts, as defined by Blumer (1954), allowing one to simplify action for purposes of interpretation—whereas in concrete terms the behavior of individuals may be exceedingly complex.

Saying an organizational action has three dimensions means that it may be viewed in three different contexts of meaning. According to John Dewey, "Perception of meanings depends upon perception of connections, of context," (1961, p.287). Thus one has a structural, typically task or economic, set of relationships and context for action. Herein the term economic is used in its broadest sense, referring to social action dealing with the material (objective) meaning of action. One has a cultural, or normative, set of relationships and (subjective) context for action. This refers to meaning assessed in terms of beliefs, values, and norms. Further, one has an administrative, or authority, set of relationships and (reflexive) context for action. Authority, or dominance, refers to the purposive subordination of some actions to other actions. Altogether, the three dimensions represent qualitatively different orientations to action, or attitudes of other, or ways of interpreting action within an organization. Thus, one may view the meaning of organizational action simultaneously in structural, economic, task related terms; in cultural, social, normative terms; and in administrative, authority, political terms. As with the metaphor of primary colors, these contexts of meaning, or analytical dimensions, are blended or combined in organizational action. However, ordinarily one dimension of meaning will dominate in an organization. As to why one dimension of meaning is dominant, and more particularly why a certain version of this meaning prevails, individuals in organizations as in societies—in aggregate action, group action, or organized action—engage in contention over which meaning is dominant. Stephen Kalberg, commenting on Weber, refers to such collectivities as "social carriers," (2012, p.117–118). Each dimension of meaning provides a medium for dissention and conflict. Conversely, each provides a medium for group or organizational cohesion and solidarity.

> Individuals in organizations as in societies—in aggregate action, group action, or organized action—engage in contention over which meaning is dominant.

The dimensions of meaning may be illustrated as follows. Consider the purchase of a house. One may purchase a house in a particular location to participate in the real estate market as an investor, to become a landlord, or to gain tax benefits. One may purchase the house to live among neighbors with high status, to express one's architectural preferences, or to be near good schools for one's children. One may purchase the house to vote in a particular jurisdiction, to qualify as a candidate for public office, or to organize a political campaign. Of course, one may do all three at the same time, as is probably true of many individuals. In an organizational context one may consider such things as whether an action is practical, effective, cost efficient, profitable, or not. One may consider whether or not it comports with the ethos, the beliefs, the values, the norms of the organization. One may consider whether or not it accords with the policies, the rules, the objectives, etc. of the organization. Naturally, the organization's leadership would probably hope all actions meet all three criteria of meaning.

The three different orientations to action may be most apparent when they come into conflict. With reference to an organization's structure, culture, and authority, an action may be effective and legal, but not moral. In banking and corporate finance one may see many examples in which the assets of small investors and retirees are depleted in an immoral but not ineffective or illegal manner. An action may be effective and moral, but not legal. Here one can think of the examples of the Underground Railroad helping African Americans escape slavery, and some forms of resistance action to protect Jews from the Holocaust. Finally, an action may be ineffective but moral and legal. Mishandled prison executions and the failed U.S. prohibition of alcohol consumption were both, at a particular time and place, legal and broadly supported. In addition, every occupational action has the possibility, if not the actuality, of such conflict. This is often the case with professionals employed in organizations dominated by orientations other than that of their profession. To successfully complete a task one may have to do things that are professionally inappropriate or other than directed by a supervisor. To do as a supervisor suggests one may have to compromise the task or do professionally inappropriate things. To do what is right by professional values one may have to ignore a superior or scuttle the task. A physician or nurse may be barred by hospital policy from providing needed services. An attorney acting as a public defender may be hampered by a heavy caseload from providing good client representation. A priest or pastor may be pressured by clerical peers into not disclosing knowledge of a sexual assault. An individual professional, or a professional group, may be pulled in different directions—what is effective, what is legal, what is moral? The actions may be seen in three different contexts, or orders of meaning.

The meaning of something in a social milieu is its presumed consequences in the course of action. This, to be sure, is the pragmatist philosophical position. John Dewey said variously:

Let us, however, follow the pragmatic rule, and in order to discover the meaning of the idea ask for its consequences. (1957, p.163)

These consequences constitute the meaning and value of an activity as it comes under deliberation. (1922, p.225)

The very conception of cognitive meaning, intellectual significance, is that things in their immediacy are subordinate to what they portend and give evidence of. (1929, p.128)

When one speaks of meaning, one speaks of consequences, ends, outcomes, results of action. Within this essay, meaning is the socially-recognized, intended consequence, or effect, of an action. Or, to someone else, what they take the relevant consequences to be. This interpretation of meaning, as said earlier, is consistent with Mead and Weber. Mead says somewhat densely:

The gesture stands for a certain result of the social act, a resultant to which there is a definite response on the part of the individual involved therein; so that meaning is given or stated in terms of response.

If that gesture does so indicate to another organism the subsequent (or resultant) behavior of the given organism, then it has that meaning. (1965, p.76)

With respect to Weber, Gerth and Mills conclude, "In his writings on method, Weber rejects the assumption of any 'objective meaning.' He wished to restrict the understanding and interpretation to the subjective intentions of the actor," (1946, p.58). The actor's intentions are, of course, the intended consequences, or anticipated outcome of action.

Weber observes that social action may vary in the extent to which it is meaningful:

Empirically fluid is the transition from the ideal type of a meaningful relationship between one's own action and that of others to the case in which another person is merely an object (for example an infant). For us, behavior that is oriented toward meaningful action is only the rational limiting case. (1978, p.1376)

Mead, of course, would agree. As previously suggested, meaning is the anticipated consequence of an action within a particular social milieu. That is, viewed in different social contexts, objectively similar action has different meaning. And, meaning varies among individuals or groups with different attitudes, who may view the consequences of action in terms of different contexts. Accordingly, within this essay the three organizational dimensions are three different contexts, or referents, for the consequences of social action, i.e., meaning. This point deserves emphasis, as it is fundamental for all that follows in this essay.

> Within this essay the three organizational dimensions are three different contexts, or referents, for the consequences of social action, i.e., meaning.

Insofar as individuals or groups are oriented in their action to one type of meaning (i.e., consequence) or another, it may be useful to have terms to refer to such orientations. For purposes of analysis, one may refer to orientations (or attitudes) toward organized action in each of the three dimensions as follows. An orientation to action and its consequences in the structural dimension is an orientation to "utilitive meaning." This relates to such things as task performance, exchange activities, establishing a division of labor, and other actions directed principally at material or economic consequences. An orientation to action and its consequences in the cultural dimension is an orientation to "normative meaning." This relates to such things as ceremonies, rituals, conferring or recognizing status, relating history, lore, and myth, and otherwise sharing or expressing beliefs, values, and norms. An orientation to action and its consequences in the authority dimension is an orientation to "authoritive meaning." This relates to such things as delegation, legitimacy, policy, rules, adjudication, conflict mediation, and other aspects of collective decision making. Looking ahead, it will become apparent that individuals strive to advance their utilitive interests, their normative ideas, and their authoritive allegiances—individually, as groups, sometimes as organized groups.

As stated earlier, in social action a greater emphasis may be placed upon task activities, cultural ideas, or authority. This makes the action principally utilitive, normative, or authoritive. Within an organization one set of relationships, characterized by a particular type of meaning, is likely to be dominant over the others. Any concrete organizational action will necessarily include all three dimensions, or orientations to action, but generally some choice must be made whether one primarily seeks utilitive, normative, or authoritive ends of action. Otherwise said, organizations will differ by being different types of meaning systems. It follows that these distinctions may be used to identify three types of organizations. These are analytic types. This is comparable to Weber's observation that there are class and status societies, and by extension also party societies. In addition, the organizational types employed in this essay are very similar those of Weber, Bell, and several other authors. As to exhibiting a dominant meaning, this accords with the fact that organizations are rational instruments. Means and ends are consciously related, and some actions are necessarily subordinated to other actions. For example, communicating ideas—beliefs, values, norms—is necessary to facilitate a utilitive task, e.g., assembling an automobile or moving a household of furniture, but expressing such ideas is a means, not the principal end, or purpose, of the task. Conversely, the performance of utilitive tasks, e.g., cleaning a hall, arranging chairs, or distributing printed materials is probably essential, a necessary means, for many cultural, or normative, actions, e.g., conducting a ceremony, delivering a lecture, preaching a sermon, or presenting a concert, but is not the principal end or general meaning of the action. At issue here is which type of action—utilitive, normative, or authoritive—will be the principal end and predominantly characterize the organization?

CHAPTER VII

Ideal Types

Organizations, or organized actions, tend to emphasize one kind of meaning—utilitive, normative, or authoritive—to the relative diminution of the others. That is, generally one orientation to action, or meaning, will be the dominant orientation among participants. In addition, the prevalence of one kind of meaning will likely be associated with distinctive organizational characteristics. One may expect the "conformation" of an organization to vary according to the prevalent meaning. The dominant meaning draws, or is drawn to, compatible patterns of social action. Accordingly, one may recognize types of organizations based on the predominant meaning associated with action. Said otherwise, one may recognize types of organizations according to the consequences that are emphasized. This agrees with Weber's view of the relationship of meaning and patterns of action. Heckman (1983) says of Weber:

> One may recognize types of organizations based on the predominant meaning associated with action ... the consequences that are emphasized.

With regard to every structural analysis that he considers, Weber
would argue that the structure would not be a particular type

unless the dominant belief system were a corresponding type; and conversely, a particular kind of belief system is manifest in a particular structure (p.57).

Weber always identifies an action by specifying its subjective meaning and by identifying the particular course of action that is linked to the meaning. Thus, it is simply not the case that meaning determines action or vice versa, rather meaning and action are linked, and both follow from identification of the action (p.51).

Later this linkage will be discussed in terms of Weber's concept of elective affinity. That is, the linkage is principally due to a consonance, or compatibility, of meanings. Likewise, Mead saw that subjective orientations to action tend to be associated with compatible patterns of action. For example, this association was underscored by Mead's concept of "universals' previously discussed.

> **Ideal types are conceptual exaggerations that are used for analysis of social action.**

The fact that the conformation, or patterns of action in organizations, tends to vary in accordance with the meaning that is dominant encourages the construction of what are called "ideal types." Herein, ideal types are qualitative concepts used for the analysis of social action. Karl Popper, noted philosopher of science, approvingly discussed methodology that is exemplified by the ideal type:

I refer to the possibility of adopting, in the social sciences, what may be called the method of logical or rational construction, or perhaps the "zero method." By this I mean the constructing of a model on the assumption of complete rationality (and perhaps also the assumption of the possession of complete information) on the part of individuals concerned, and of estimating the deviation of the actual behavior of people from the model behavior, using the latter as a kind of zero coordinate. (1989, p.141)

An ideal type is a limiting concept, which is presumed to normally be unattainable, but nevertheless is useful as a comparative standard. With regard to social action one can think of several examples such as perfectly rational economic action, perfect adherence to religious standards, or perfect compliance with laws and rules of society. Examples of ideal types from other contexts are a perfect vacuum, absolute zero temperature, or the speed of light. These are thought to normally be unattainable, but useful as standards for comparison.

Max Weber was, without question, the greatest proponent of using ideal type concepts in social analysis. Ideal types were constructed and used to great effect by Weber in his analysis of factors contributing to the distinctive character of Western Civilization. For example, he identified types of governance, types of economic organization, and types of religious behavior. Weber's preferred method for analyzing the interplay of ideas and patterns of action, as well as forms of legitimate power, is the ideal type. A particularly influential ideal type formulated by Weber is his concept of bureaucracy. This concept has set the terms of debate in much of the literature on organizations. Some of the other ideal types formulated by Weber, as previously mentioned, are traditional, rational, and charismatic authority; class, status group, and party; and economic, status, and legal orders in society. Another example of the use of ideal types in sociological analysis is that of Daniel Bell, in his discussion of "post-industrial society":

> *The post-industrial society, as I have emphasized several times, is primarily a change of social structure—in a dimension, not of the total configuration of society. It is an "ideal type," a construct, put together by the social analyst, of diverse changes in the society which, when assembled, become more or less coherent when contrasted with other conceptual constructs. (1973, p.487)*

There are many other examples of ideal types in the sociological literature, such as Tonnies' "community" and "society," and Durkheim's "mechanical" and "organic solidarity." Examples of ideal types in organizational literature, include Ritzer's "McDonalization," Burns and Stalker's "Mechanistic' and "Organic" organizations, McGregor's "Theory X" and "Theory Y," and Ouchi's "Theory Z." None of these organizations exist as factual entities; the authors claim that only approximations exist. Yet, these authors consider these concepts useful for making meaningful theoretical statements. The ideal types are useful for analysis and comparison of organizations.

As said, ideal types are conceptual exaggerations that are used for analysis of social action. An ideal type is a highly abstract rendition of a possible course of action, presented in its purest, unadulterated form. An ideal type draws out and emphasizes in the extreme the essential characteristics of a rational course of action. According to Swedberg, "For methodological convenience, Weber argues, sociology should start out by constructing what a rational action would look like—then attempt to explain deviations from this." (2005, p.223). In Weber's own words:

> *For purposes of systematic scientific analysis it will be convenient to represent all irrational, emotionally conditioned elements of conduct as deviations from a conceptually pure type of goal-oriented behavior… The construction of a purely rational goal-oriented course of conduct, because of its clear understandability and rational unambiguity, serves sociology as an "ideal type."… Naturally, this procedure may not be interpreted as a rationalistic bias on the part of sociology, but simply as a methodological device. (1993, p.32)*

Any particular ideal type may be useful, or it may be irrelevant, to the analysis of a particular social event. Actual behavior is compared to the ideal type to see in what respect it corresponds with the ideal type, the manner in which it deviates from the pure form of action, and the orientations to action associated with these patterns of deviation. Ideal types are not hypotheses; they are not subject to validation or invalidation by empirical data. Therefore, the considerable literature attempting to validate or invalidate Weber's ideal types, casting them as hypotheses, is misdirected. Unfortunately, many notable American scholars attempted to test the validity of Weber's ideal types once they became translated mid-Twentieth Century. In so doing, they imputed to his works a misplaced positivism. In addition, ideal types are not constituted for descriptive purposes. They are deliberate exaggerations. Heckman explains the strength of the ideal type methodology, as used by Weber:

> *The relevance of the synthesis that Weber effects in the ideal type lies in the fact that, on the one hand, it is firmly rooted in the social actor's subjective meaning and, on the other hand, without losing this subjective grounding, it provides a tool for the structural analysis of social institutions. (1983, p.15)*

One may attempt to put the ideal type in the phraseology of Mead. The ideal type rendered in Mead's terms would simply be a pattern of action predicated on a perfectly reflexive attitude of other, or generalized other. Again, it does not and cannot exist in actual practice. Borrowing Blumer's term, ideal types are useful as "sensitizing concepts." They are not used mechanically, but as lanterns to illuminate things, make noticeable what might otherwise be unnoticed, unobserved. They suggest what to look for in a given situation.

Due to the importance of ideal types to this essay, a recap of the preceding discussion may be of use. An ideal type is simply a very abstract rendering of some kind of general social action, which consists of two things. One is the expression of a single-minded, sole objective, or meaning of a type of action. The other is the characteristic set, or pattern, of activities which make up this qualitative type and are motivated only by the singular objective, or meaning. Further, the whole is idealized as a perfectly reflexive, or rational, form of action. Thus, all aspects of the ideal type action are entirely consistent with the objective, or meaning. When one says rational, one doesn't mean objectively rational. One means strictly goal directed, or a single-minded course of action—subjectively rational. Accordingly, the abstraction can be used as a standard for analytic purposes. One looks at real action—presently, in retrospect, or as anticipated—to see in what ways it corresponds or deviates from the idealized course of action. One can, of course, follow this procedure with several idealized models at the same time, assessing the apparent, relative influence of several orientations to action. In Mead's lexicon, these would be competing attitudes of other. All of this is very malleable, as one can repeatedly adjust the idealized models of action, seek new evidence to test the models, and in particular look for critical evidence that tests one model pitted against another. Such tests would likely be what Mead terms "significant gestures" or "significant symbols' which unambiguously display the meaning of action. And, a test could be described as what Weber called a 'mental experiment," (1946, p.169; 1978, p.919). It should be added that all of this is what individuals normally do in everyday life when exercising reflexive intelligence. For example, one says to oneself that another person, if he or she has a particular intention, will likely do a certain thing. Conversely, if that person does a certain thing, he or she likely has a particular intention. Then, one may inquire, or simply watch for a pattern of action to test the supposition.

Theorists often find it meaningful to place organizations into typological classifications. Several theorists and their classifications have already been mentioned in this essay. The discussion now turns to those theorists who are particularly relevant here. Amitai Etzioni classifies organizations according to three types, "utilitarian," "normative," and "coercive" based on the kind of compliance that is dominant in an organization (1961, p.xvi). Etzioni says:

> *Compliance is a relationship consisting of the power employed by superiors to control subordinates and the orientation of subordinates to this power (p.xv).*

The assumption… is that there are three major sources of control,
whose allocation and manipulation account to a great extent
for the foundations of social order (p.xvi).

Power is of three kinds: "economic assets," "normative values," and "coercion." Etzioni asserts that type of compliance is related to many other organizational variables, such as goals, elites, communication, consensus, and the allocation of tasks and power (p.xv, p.27–44). In comparing organizations he takes into account which power is predominant, how strongly it is stressed, and which power is the secondary source of control. Most organizations employ all three types of power to some extent. Typical examples of coercive organizations are: concentration camps, prisons, and custodial mental hospitals. Examples of utilitarian organizations are: blue collar, white collar, and, in part, professional organizations. Examples of normative organizations are: religious, general hospital, and university organizations. However, Etzioni sets himself apart from Weber and ideal types in what is simply a positivistic misreading of Weber, but his observations are nonetheless very useful.

Peter B. Clarke (1961, passim) and James Q. Wilson (1995, p.30–51) produced an analysis of political organizations that lies very close to the perspective of this essay. The analysis was originally a joint article, but it was later expanded into a book by Wilson. They recognize three types of organizations, each sustained by a particular type of incentive (or meaning) offered to members. "Utilitarian" organizations rely primarily on tangible, "material incentives" that have monetary value. "Solidary" organizations (with two variations, individual and collective) are based primarily on "intangible incentives" that arise out of the act of "associating." "Purposive" organizations primarily use "intangible incentives" in the form of satisfaction gained from contributing to the attainment of a worthwhile cause. In the Clarke-Wilson schema the dominant type of incentive, or reward, used by an organization defines the character of the organization, but most organizations use a combination of incentives. Wilson states explicitly that the analysis employs ideal types (p.35). He says, "Though examples will be drawn from existing organizations, it should be understood that here one is dealing with ideal types—organizations that (unrealistically) depend entirely on a single, distinctive incentive." Their analysis presents an ideal-typical classification of organizations that exhibits a sound understanding of Weber's concepts and methods. However, the Clarke-Wilson classification schema assumes an exchange relationship between member and organization and an equilibrium model of organizations. Neither is fully compatible with Weber's perspective as it is interpreted within this essay. In this essay relationships may be a matter of exchange, but also communal or authority relations, and this difference is consequential. Further, organizations do not fit an equilibrium model, but are assumed to be in a contentious process of reconstruction, with strong emergent properties.

Richard Scott recognized three perspectives on organizations, "rational," "natural," and "open," which appear to largely correspond to the authoritive, normative, and utilitive distinctions in this essay (1998, p.24–29). According to Scott, the rational system definition views organizations as "oriented to the pursuit of relatively specific goals and exhibiting relatively highly formalized social structures," (p.26). This corresponds to the characteristics of this essay's authoritive type. The rational system emphasizes such things as hierarchy, authority, and various attributes of rational control. In contrast, the natural system definition views organizations as having participants who pursue multiple interests, "but recognize the value of perpetuating the organization as an important resource," (p.26). And, informal relations are more important than formal relations in understanding organizational behavior. The natural system emphasizes such things as cooperation, community, informal structure, personal relations, consensus, and values. It obviously corresponds to the characteristics of this essay's normative type. Thirdly, the open systems perspective emphasizes such things as exchange, external relations, operations (at a production or task level), and in-puts and out-puts. Scott says organizations in the open systems definition:

> *[A]re open to and dependent upon flows of personnel, resources, and information from the outside... Individuals have multiple loyalties and identities. They join and leave or engage in ongoing exchanges with the organization depending upon the bargain they can strike—the relative advantage to be had from maintaining or ending the relation. (p.27)*

Furthermore, open system "organizations are systems of interdependent activities," (p.28). Open systems are viewed as heavily dependent upon exchanges with their environments, or one could say they are market-oriented. This clearly corresponds to the economic and exchange aspects of this essay's utilitive ideal type. Altogether, the three perspectives on organizations that Scott described are comparable to the three ideal types of organizations considered in this essay.

William Ouchi presented a theory of organizations, Theory Z, in response to McGregor's Theory X and Theory Y. Together, these three concepts may be viewed as similar to the normative, authoritive, and utilitive ideal types in this essay. Ouchi recounts, "A Theory X manager assumes that people are fundamentally lazy, irresponsible and need to be watched. A Theory Y manager assumes that people are fundamentally hard-working, responsible, and need only to be supported and encouraged," (1981, p.69). One may suggest that the Theory X organization, placing a large emphasis upon the exercise of authority, has some commonality with this essay's authoritive type. The Theory Y organization places an emphasis upon task performance and an enabling setting for task performance. Thus, it appears the Theory Y organization has some commonality with this essay's utilitive ideal type.

Ouchi's Theory Z organization, based on his study of Japanese firms, clearly corresponds to this essay's normative ideal type. The Theory Z organization emphasizes culture and "clan," or community relations, within a business organization. Ouchi contrasts Type Z with a bureaucracy:

> *The difference between a hierarchy—or bureaucracy—and Type Z is that organizations have achieved a high state of consistency in their internal culture. They are most aptly described as clans in that they are intimate associations of people engaged in economic activity but tied together through a variety of bonds. (p.83)*

Ouchi also says, "The coordination in the system is provided by adherence to an underlying set of values that are deeply held and closely followed." (p.89). Further, "The only way to influence behavior is to change the culture." (p.88). However, according to Ouchi, the clan form of organization, Theory Z, has some notable limitations:

> *Despite its remarkable properties, the clan form in industry possesses a few disabling weaknesses. A clan always tends to develop xenophobia, a fear of outsiders... In other ways, too, the Type Z resists deviance in all forms. Because the glue that holds it together is consistency of belief rather than application of hierarchy, it tends indiscriminately to reject all inconsistency. (p.88)*

For later reference, this emphasis on a normative orientation, and the associated xenophobia, serve to bring forward status group characteristics.

According to the systems theorists Katz and Kahn (1965):

> *Society is sustained (1) through the rewards of its economic system, which provide powerful instrumental motivation toward socially-required behaviors; (2) by the maintenance structures of education and religion, which inculcate the general norms and specific behavioral codes; and (3) by the political structures which pass and enforce laws. (p.113)*

> *These three major types of integration are a more complex expression of the three bases of social systems: (1) task requirements in relation to needs, (2) shared values and norms, and (3) rule enforcement. (p.113)*

> *These major tasks are distributed among organizations which generally specialize in a single function but make supplementary contributions in other areas. (p.113)*

> *Almost every organization tends to employ all three bases to ensure effective performance, but the relative emphasis upon the them varies greatly from organization to organization, with industrial enterprises at one extreme and voluntary organizations at the other. (p.119)*

Thus, Katz and Kahn have identified three functional requirements to maintain an organization within a social system. And, greater emphasis upon one functional requirement gives rise to a corresponding type of organization. However, apparently in an effort to adapt their model to Talcott Parson's four-part functional systems theory (AGIL), Katz and Kahn belatedly append a fourth organizational dimension. In the three-function mode, the Katz and Kahn perspective is remarkably similar to the ideal type constructs in this essay. However, this essay does not accept the assumptions of a functionalist systems approach, nor the AGIL model.

Each of the foregoing perspectives on organizations brings forth a tri-part typology. And, in one manner or another, each of these typologies can be placed in the utilitive—normative—authoritive framework. As such they express the structural, cultural, and authority dimensions discussed earlier in this essay. And, they comport with the "orders" of Weber, the "early universals" of Mead, and the "realms" of Bell. It would appear that an answer to Donaldson's "paradigm proliferation," the futility of disconnected organizational theories, may lie within these distinctions. As suggested previously in the story of the three blind men and the elephant, many organizational theories emphasize one dimension, one perspective on organizations, to the exclusion or diminution of others. That, of course, is not true of the perspectives recounted above, but it appears to be true of much of the organizational literature—hence the proliferation of disparate theories. This essay will suggest that organized action, or organizations, may be more effectively, more productively studied by explicitly, deliberately recognizing all three dimension of organizational action. If one seeks the interpretation of action in terms of its subjective meaning, as Weber suggests one should do, then one must pay attention to all dimensions of meaning in organized action. In Mead's terms, one must strive to be fully reflexive, incorporate all three generic attitudes of other, in the examination of organizations and individuals' participation in organizations.

Perhaps it would be useful at this point of the essay to illustrate what is meant by the different types of organizations. One does so, however, recognizing that the purpose of ideal types is not description of concrete entities. It is quite possible to place a real organization in a particular category, in which it nominally belongs, but find on closer examination that its dominant traits belong to another classification. Thus, one could have a college or university, putatively holding a normative orientation, which actually functions as a predatory utilitive organization. Or, one could have a trade union that ostensibly serves as a utilitive organization for its members, but in fact works to advance the agenda of a subversive political party. In such cases, as in all cases, one must go beyond labels and analyze the patterns of action and the objectives that are consistently sought. With these caveats in mind one may nonetheless illustrate the three ideal type organizations, doing so in very general terms, and being mindful that the illustrations are only suggestive.

There are no purely utilitive, normative, or authoritive organizations. In daily life there are only organizations that are predominantly of one type or another, that exhibit one quality more than the others. They exhibit a prevalence of exchange, communal, or authority relations, respectively. Otherwise said, such organizations will differ by being different types of meaning systems. The type of meaning that is dominant will vary between organizations and within organizations. This difference in dimensional dominance will be expressed in structural differences, will be a source of conflict, and will be a key to comparative analysis of organized action. For illustrative purposes, consider the following list of organizations with presumably a greater emphasis on the utilitive dimension: a business union, an entrepreneurial business, a for-profit college or training institute, a proprietary hospital, a Catholic winery, and a mercenary military unit. Organizations with presumably a greater emphasis on the normative dimension may include: a social or professional union, a cooperative or hobby business, a liberal arts college, a community hospital, a Catholic parochial school, and a special military unit, e.g., Seals. Organizations with presumably a greater emphasis on the authoritive dimension may include: a Communist Party or mob-controlled union, a cartel or monopoly business, a military college, a military veterans hospital, a Catholic diocese, and a regular military unit. Again, these examples are only for purpose of illustration. Recall that the stated purpose of ideal types is not descriptive accuracy but as an aid to analysis. The suggestion here is that ideal types are a heuristic device. Ideal types are simply concepts for refracting, or combing out, the dimensions of meaning—separating the threads that make up the social fabric. Their use is in abstracting a meaningful interpretation of social events.

One may reasonably ask why an emphasis upon a particular type of subjective meaning will tend to be associated with particular, objective, organizational characteristics, or what this essay refers to as the conformation of the organization. Within this essay such association is not assumed to be a product of positivistic causes. Positivism is emphatically rejected. Rather, one may think of it as a matter of cognitive consonance, as opposed to a dissonance of attitudes and actions. Types appear to exist because, upon emphasizing one dimension of meaning, this draws compatible forms of social action, or vice versa. Said otherwise, one may think of the association as a sensible relation between the means and ends of social action. Very simply, in meaningful behavior the means of action will be expected to accord with the ends of action. As has been mentioned previously, in Weber's lexicon it's a matter of elective affinity. According to Gerth and Mills, "The decisive conception by which Weber relates ideas and interests is that of 'elective affinity,' rather than 'correspondence,' 'reflection,' or 'expression,'" (1946, p.62). Translated into the terminology, herein, it is the decisive conception by which culture (ideas) and structure (interests) are related—and one must add authority, as well. One could say that elective affinity is the glue that holds social action together.

It is one aspect of Weber's emphasis upon *verstehen*, or meaning, in interpreting social action, and more will be said about elective affinity later in this essay. Briefly, what organizational characteristics should one expect to vary in accordance with differences in predominant meaning. One may expect that dimensional dominance will be related to such things as the type of elite in control of the organization, which organizational

> Elective affinity is the glue that holds social action together.

needs are given greater resources, which problems will be given priority, the best route for mobility in the organization, the type of environmental relations that are paramount, where structural enhancement will likely occur, and so on.

The ideal type methodology espoused by Weber is entirely consistent with the symbolic interactionist approach rising largely from the work of George H. Mead. Mead's student and colleague Herbert Blumer was the leading interpreter of Mead's work. As previously mentioned, Blumer (1954) stated, "I think that the concepts of our discipline are fundamentally 'sensitizing concepts.'" We need "sensitizing concepts" because "what we are referring to by any concept shapes up in a different way in each empirical instance." It is the nature of symbols that, while the objective particulars may vary, the subjective meaning may remain the same. Blumer further says, "It gives the user a general sense of reference and guidance in approaching empirical instances. Whereas definitive concepts provide prescriptions of what to see, sensitizing concepts merely suggest directions along which to look." The point is not to use concepts mechanically, but as a means to illuminate things, make noticeable what would otherwise remain unobserved. They suggest what to look for in identifying the meaning of action and, therefore, in constructing a meaningful interpretation of social action.

The comparability of Weber's ideal types and sensitizing concepts in symbolic interaction has not gone unnoticed. Craig observes, "Weber… referred to these theoretical reference points as ideal types. The symbolic interactionist Herbert Blumer… proposed a related idea of sensitizing concepts," (2013, p.50–51). Hendricks speaks of "sensitizing concepts that support the process of clarification and interpretation. They are 'ideal types,'" (2010, p.179). Brekhus (2015) cites the use of "sensitizing analytic concepts for thinking about social classification… ideal type strategies for classification." Rosenthal notes how in a similar manner sensitizing concepts and ideal types provide guidance for sociological analysis (2012, p.203).

> In a similar manner sensitizing concepts and ideal types provide guidance for sociological analysis.

This comparability of ideal types and sensitizing concepts is yet another example of the correspondence of Mead and Weber's theories. And it further shows how Weber's concepts may be borrowed by symbolic interaction to deal with large-scale social interaction, meso- and macro-sociology. With this in mind, discussion now turns to considering the origins of collective action, within and without organizations. Inasmuch as organizations differ according to dominant meaning, how is it this dominance and its form of expression is established? That is, the discussion turns to the consideration of class, status group, and party forms of action. These, or their similitudes, are the contenders in the struggle over dominant meaning in organizations.

CHAPTER IIX.

Class

This essay has discussed how the prevalent meaning of action varies among organizations, thereby allowing the distinction of three different types of organizations, referred to as the utilitive organization, the normative organization, and the authoritive organization. It has also mentioned that these types may be comparable to Weber's class, status, and (additionally) party societies. Attention now turns to how meaning attributed to action varies within organizations. That is, the individuals participating in an organization, regardless of organizational type, do not all have the same material interests, the same beliefs, values, and norms, or the same allegiance to organizational authority. Said otherwise, they do not all have the same utilitive, normative, or authoritive attitudes concerning organizational participation. Yet, these differences among individuals, regardless of organizational type, are not randomly or arbitrarily distributed. Rather, they are largely distributed according to collectivities, or groupings of individuals, within an organization. That is, in any organization one may distinguish a number of collectivities with characteristically different utilitive attitudes, a number of collectivities with characteristically different normative attitudes, and a number of collectivities with characteristically different authoritive attitudes. And, this distribution underlies an endless struggle among various collectivities over the type of meaning and the manner of expression that dominates in an organization. The struggle is usually complex, inasmuch as individual participants in an organization typically belong to a number of such collectivities. To understand this struggle, one may first consider how ideas about meaning differ among groupings of individuals within society at large. In so doing, discussion will focus on sensitizing concepts, or ideal types, that later will be useful in discussing collective action within organizations.

Weber observed that the distribution of different attitudes toward social action has architecture within societies. At the most general level, as previously mentioned, it is according to orders. He mentions three orders, and each order features a different type of meaning, or qualitatively different set of prescriptions for social action. One may recall that Weber distinguished the following orders: economic, social, and legal. As previously mentioned, Weber's orders are comparable to Mead's early universals and Bell's realms in society. Weber's orders are also comparable to the dimensions of meaning discussed throughout this essay—the primary colors of social action. In addition to representing different types of orientation to action, or meaning, each order presents a different mode of social stratification. In fact, the classic, most influential approach to social stratification in sociology is that of Weber. In this stratification each order harbors a distinctive type of collectivity, or grouping: classes reside in the economic order; status groups reside in the social order (or cultural order); and parties reside in the legal order (or authority order). Each collectivity within an order maintains a particular version of that order's type of meaning. Thus, in the economic order different classes tend to have different material interests and characteristically different utilitive orientations to action. In the status order different status groups tend to have cultural differences, or what Weber referred to as "ideal interests." Thus, they may have different beliefs, values, and norms—or different normative orientations to action. In the legal order, or what this essay has termed the authority order, parties or party-like groupings reflect different allegiances, or authoritive orientations to action. Recall that parties are oriented to different dispositions and use of authority.

Each class, status group, or party tends to occupy a distinctive place, or standing within its order—typically there is some stratification. However, and this will be revisited, it may be horizontal as well as vertical stratification. In that these concepts—class, status group, and party—are central to this essay, one should consider Weber's (1978) own words:

> *Whereas the genuine place of classes is within the economic order, the place of status groups is within the social order, that is within the sphere of the distribution of honor. From within these spheres, classes and status groups influence one another and the legal order and are in turn influenced by it. (p.938)*

Parties reside in the sphere of power. Their action is oriented toward the acquisition of social power, that is to say, toward influencing social action no matter what its content may be. In principle, parties may exist in a social club as well as a state. As over against the action of classes and status groups, for which this is not necessarily the case, party-oriented action always involves association. For it is always directed toward a goal which is striven for in a planned manner. (p.938)

A clarification, when one speaks of "honor" associated with status groups, this refers not only to prestige but more importantly a code of honor, the behavior of members in good standing—or as Weber calls it, a "style of life." In addition, when speaking of power within an association (organization) one is ultimately speaking of legitimate power, authority. In the terms used in this essay, classes are a feature of structural relationships, status groups are a feature of cultural relationships, and parties are a feature of authority relationships. In sum, within each of the three orders, the stratified collectivities or groupings have different perspectives on that order's type of meaning, different relative standing in terms of that meaning, and different inclinations toward collective action.

Weber recognized that parties may exist in everyday organizations, as well as in societies, however inchoate or well-defined a party may be. He says:

Parties may have an ephemeral character or may be organized with a view to permanent activity. They may appear in all types of organizations and may themselves be organized in any one of a large variety of forms… By definition a party can exist only within an organization, in order to influence its policy or gain control of it. (p.284–285)

This essay will assert that, by extension, if Weber recognized parties within organizations, formations of class, or class-like, and status group, or status group-like collectivities may be inferred, as well. This follows from the existence of parties in organizations, and, as later discussed, that parties are generally based on class and status, or material and ideal interests (p.938). In addition, it is reasonable to postulate that the same, or similar, collective forces that exist in society, at large, exist within organizations, which are a part of society. Undoubtedly most individuals know from personal experience, if not otherwise, that what are here described as class interests, status affinities, and party loyalties of every possible description frequently make their way into organizations. Further, one may assume that orders—class orders, social (or status) orders, and legal (or authority) orders—exist within organizations, again however well or ill defined.

In simpler terms, the orders are the economic structure (or task and exchange relations), the dominant culture (beliefs, values, norms), and the prevailing authority (or administrative) arrangements within an organization. With reference to societies Weber used the terms economic, social, and legal orders. Herein, with reference to common organizations, the comparable terms are utilitive, normative, and authoritive orders. Each order serves in its own way to restrain, or delimit, the variability of individual and group action. In accord with Weber, one may say that classes, or class-like aggregates of individuals, are situated in the task and exchange relations, or utilitive order. Status, or status-like, groups are situated in the cultural relations of an organization, or normative order. Parties, or party-like formations of organized action, are situated in the authority relations, or authoritive order. With respect to an individual, class is one's classification in an aggregate of individuals with common task and exchange relations, status is where one stands among cultural or subcultural groups, and party is one's partisanship in organized action to influence authority. However, it is necessary to again state that these terms are put forward as sensitizing concepts, analogous to Weber's ideal types, and are not empirical claims, as such. Whatever their validity as factual entities, and this essay assumes they have a real, if mutable, validity in organizations, their purpose is to serve as guides in the interpretation of organizational action.

The terms class, status group, and party are often viewed as concepts that simply denote different modalities of vertical stratification, or vertical layering in society. However, in this essay stratification means horizontal as well as vertical comparative positioning. But more important, as demonstrated in Weber's various studies, class, status group, and party are not merely ways of describing relative position in society. They are powerful analytic concepts for identifying and mentally separating and assessing the principal forces in collective action.

> Class, status group, and party ... are powerful analytic concepts for identifying and mentally separating and assessing the principal forces in collective action.

For example, in Weber's best known work, The Protestant Ethic and the Spirit of Capitalism, one may observe that Calvinist Protestants are a religious status group and Capitalists are an economic class. Other examples could be drawn from Weber's numerous studies of the interaction of religious, economic, and political forces in a broad range of societies. He demonstrated repeatedly that the concepts of class, status group, and party may be used to pull apart the layers or dimensions of meaning in complex social action. This may be done to understand the actions that made up a historical event, to analytically compare two or more patterns of action, and so on. As previously mentioned, this is somewhat analogous to using a glass prism to refract light into the various colors that compose it, and then doing spectral analysis. To cite a contemporary example, one may observe that a political coalition, perhaps the organized support for a particular piece of legislation in congress, generally draws support from a diverse array of groups: some based principally on class interests, some based principally on status group values, and some based principally on political party ambitions. Additionally, one may observe that congress is an organization.

Karl Marx saw societies and the course of history shaped primarily by a struggle among economic classes. However, in his specific historical studies he often recognized the influence of social and political factors, as well. Seymour Martin Lipset notes, for example, that when writing of the limited prospects for socialism in America, Marx did not just consider economic factors, but considered the effects of culture and democratic government (1997, p.79). Similar to Marx, Weber believed individuals in economic classes, acting according to their material interests, are principal shapers of societies and history. However, Weber also viewed commitments to cultural ideas and the quest to hold or influence authority as important in forming social action. Weber saw status groups as the "bearers of conventions," (1978, p.935-936). That is, it is principally status groups that convey culture—ideas, or more specifically beliefs, values, and norms. Further, status groups frequently struggle for the advancement or dominance of their ideas. In contrast, classes, as simple aggregates of individuals with common material interest—and no necessity of a sense of community—do not carry ideas, as such. However, they do have great effect—perhaps the greatest effect in the long run—as the cumulative action of individuals. In addition, classes may underlie the action of status groups or parties. For example, the members of a profession, a status group, may also have common class interests by virtue of similar employment. As for parties, they regularly appeal to class interests or status group ideal interests for support of their actions. Parties also appeal to the political interests of a cadre of activists to maintain cadre loyalty.

Bendix makes reference to Weber's views on the separate effects of ideas, economic interests, and political interests in the following passage. The passage relates to Weber's rejection of a narrow focus on material interests and structural explanations by some theorists of the time:

> *But the relative independence of ideas could be recognized, in his judgment, without either denying or neglecting the influence of political and economic interests on the development of ideas… Clearly, Weber wanted to see both lines of inquiry receive their due share of attention. (1977, p.46)*

Speaking analytically, classes, status groups, and parties are sources of collective action. However, this must be placed in the context of methodological individualism. Classes, status groups, and parties do not act, in and of themselves. It is the constituent individuals who act, and the general effect is a result of their individual actions. However, classes, status groups, and parties are useful concepts for understanding their collective action.

The general framework, herein, is that the conceptual apparatus used by Weber to study societies and institutions is also relevant to the study of everyday organizations. It is also entirely compatible with the symbolic interactionism of Mead and Blumer. Concepts of class, status group, and party—or their partial equivalents—can guide the analysis of collective action of and within commonplace organizations. Again, they are ideal types, or sensitizing concepts. Thus, with regard to interpreting collective action within societies or organizations one may look for the interplay of economic classes, cultural status groups, and political party organizations. Class, status group, and party—or class-like, status group-like, and party-like collectivities— represent the different dimensions of meaning as they appear in collective action. This is the case whether the organization is a private association or a nation state. Recalling Blumer's comment on sensitizing concepts, and adding ideal types as well, one must note that their referent will vary from one context to another. As previously mentioned, they will vary from one context to another in the fullness of their expression. In addition, they may be exclusive, or unique, to a particular organization, or they may be extensions of such collectivities in the broader society. As in the case of society at large, they may be manifest or latent as to their effect on action. That is, they may provide either an actual or a potential basis for collective action.

> Class, status group, and party ... represent the different dimensions of meaning as they appear in collective action.

If one is not comfortable with class as an analytic term within organizations, one may speak of different economic situations, different collective interests, different material conditions, so long as one means aggregates, each containing individuals with common interests. If one is not comfortable with status group as an analytic term within organizations, one may speak of identity groups, subculture groups, reference groups, as warranted, so long as one means groups of individuals with distinctive ideas and recognized standing. If one is not comfortable with party as an analytic term within organizations, one may speak of political factions, caucuses, schisms, blocks, so long as one means a group of individuals, organized or somewhat organized, attempting to gain or influence authority. However, in the above examples, one is speaking generically of classes, status groups, and parties. The narrative will continue as such in this essay. In any case, the interest is not in classes, status groups, or parties as entities. The point is to use these concepts to identify and pull apart the different strands of meaningful action within organizations.

> The point is to use these concepts to identify and pull apart the different strands of meaningful action within organizations.

One may see classes, status groups, and parties as generative of particular forms of collective action. This is both action within organizations and external action of organizations. So, within the present section of this essay the discussion has covered how organizations not only differ from other organizations in the type of meaning they emphasize, thereby allowing the construction of ideal type organizations, but they also tend to have internal distributions, different versions of meaning, according to classes, status groups, and parties. One may focus on these collectivities as sensitizing concepts, concepts to identify the collective actions that contend over the identity and the priorities of an organization.

Class as an ideal type may be used to analyze the role of economic interests in collective action. However, what is meant by class or class-like aggregates of individuals? The term class, in non-technical language, essentially refers to an individual's position in the economy of an organization, or in an organization's environment. All organizations, however non-economic they may be, have some established patterns of action for "getting things done." That is, there tends to be some task structure, or division of labor, etc., however rudimentary. In addition, there will be related ways of exchanging or distributing values. These may be explicit or implicit. Thus, individuals who occupy similar positions in a task structure, and by extension in exchange relationships, and who thereby face similar practical conditions and outcomes, may be said to have common objective interests. Their common position and common interests may be related to such things as the type of compensation, the conditions under which tasks are performed, or any number of other considerations related to the structure of tasks. In some manner they will experience similar material consequences by virtue of their similar forms of participation. According to Weber, "'Class situation' and 'class' refer only to the same (or similar) interests that an individual shares with others," (1978, p.302). Weber further states, "According to our terminology, the factor that creates 'class' is unambiguously economic interest, and indeed, only those interests involved in the existence of a market," (p.928). Thus, with respect to commonplace organizations, there is not only the importance of interests associated with task performance, but also the presence of an exchange relationship. However, one should note that class, as a concept, is not restricted to employment or profit-making situations. It is extended, here, to any organizational circumstance involving an allocation of tasks and the provision of utilities—for personal benefit or as resources used during participation.

This essay has repeatedly pointed out that a class is not a group, but an aggregate of individuals. Weber declares, "In any case, a class does not in itself constitute a group (Gemeinschaft)," (p.930). He also says, "In our terminology, 'classes' are not communities; they merely represent possible, and frequent, bases for social action," (p.927). That is, members of a class may, or may not, recognize their common identity and common interests. Weber states, "Thus, every class may be the carrier of any one of the innumerable forms of class action, but this is not necessarily so," (p.930). The following statements clarify Weber's interpretation of class:

> *Nevertheless, the concept of class-interest is an ambiguous one: even as an empirical concept as soon as one understands by it something other than the factual direction of interests following with a certain probability from the class situation for a certain average of those people subjected to the class situation. (p.928–929)*

> *For however different life chances may be, this fact in itself, according to all experience, by no means gives birth to "class action" (social action by members of a class). For that, the*

real conditions and the results of the class situation must be distinctly recognizable. (p.929)

The class situation may be restricted in its efforts to the generation of essentially similar reactions, that is to say, within our terminology, of "mass behavior." However, it may not even have this result. Furthermore, often merely amorphous social action emerges. (p.929)

However, social action that brings forth class situations is not basically action among members of the identical class; it is an action among members of different classes. (p.930)

Class aggregates may, or may not, be exclusive to an organization. Individuals within an organization may belong to aggregates with common interests extending into the organization from an outside institution or from the general society. And, inasmuch as individuals may occupy positions in a number of task structures, an individual may have a number of class situations and a plurality of class interests. Again, the focus is not on classes as things, but as analytical concepts for understanding social action. Nonetheless, for purposes of illustration, what are some examples of possible classes within organizations? Some examples of aggregates with possible common interests are: individuals with similar tasks, similar compensation, similar schedules, and similar working conditions. The point is that any such aggregation, in a particular situation, in a particular organization, could have common material interests, perhaps such as would promote some form of similar or common action. Possible forms of action might include: a slow down, shoddy performance, a walkout or wildcat strike, sabotage, absenteeism, or widespread resignations. On the positive side they might include: a high level of satisfaction, greater productivity, longevity in positions, a positive safety record, and less wastage. In addition, shared interests may lead to common support or opposition to union organizing campaigns.

CHAPTER IX

Status Group

Status groups, as an ideal type concept, may be used to analyze the role of ideas in collective action. Bendix states in regard to Weber's theoretical work, "A concept had to be formulated that would encompass the influence of ideas upon the formation of groups without losing sight of economic conditions," (1977, p.86). That is, in addition to the ideal type concept of class, a concept such as status group is necessary. Status group, however, is a concept with complex characteristics. Status group is an English translation of the German term *stand*. As Parsons noted:

> *The term* stand *with its derivatives is perhaps the most troublesome single term in Weber's text. It refers to a group the members of which occupy a relatively well-defined common status, particularly with reference to social stratification, though this reference is not always important. In addition to common status, there is the further criterion that the members of a* Stand *have a common mode of life and usually more of less well-defined "code of behavior." (1946, p.347n)*

It becomes apparent that common mode of life, or life style, and code of behavior can be interpreted as a group culture—and behavior expressing that culture. An additional distinction is also important. Whereas classes are aggregates of individuals, and parties are organizations, status collectivities are groups. Weber affirms, "In contrast to classes, *Stande* (status groups) are normally groups. They are, however, often of an amorphous kind," (1978, p.932). Some common types of status groups in present society include ethnic, religious, gender-based, age-based, sexual preference, regional, and professional groups. More particularly, one may mention Irish-American, Protestant, women's, millennial, gay, Yankee, and physician's groups. This is true insofar as they are socially recognized, somewhat cohesive groups, with distinctive ideas. With regard to distinctive ideas, consider the case of ethnic groups. Such groups often have particular beliefs, values, and norms about cuisine, mode of dress, literature, music, art, ceremonies and rituals, education, preferred occupations, leisure activities, and any number of other things. In addition, such groups—or rather the members of such groups— tend to struggle for recognition and dominance of their ideas, and, hence, are appropriately called status groups.

The status groups that have an impact on action within organizations may, or may not, be exclusive to the organizations. Status groups from the general society are often important within an organization. The examples cited above would likely be groups extending from and influencing an organization from the outside. However, status groups that are confined to an organization may be important to understanding organizational action. Examples could include organizational veterans or old-timers, novices, in-group, out-group, and legacy or non-legacy individuals. The struggle of status groups in organizations may be seen in such things as a battle of young Turks against an old guard, a protest by an ethnic minority against some form of alleged discrimination, a collective action by women to break through the glass ceiling, and contention over an office celebration of a religious holiday. Struggles between line and staff, between different departments, may be over interests or authority, but they may also be disputes among groups of individuals with different professional or craft ideas. Anticipating a later discussion, how does one assess which it is? Briefly, with ideal types as guides, one looks for patterns in the action and also interprets relevant communications. Upon observing that organizational action appears to match, or partially match, the characteristics of one of more ideal types, thereby suggesting a meaningful interpretation, or an alternative interpretation, of the action one further seeks out critical tests, watershed information, to confirm or refute any such explanations.

Status groups, as previously mentioned, are associated with a sense of honor. Weber says, "In contrast to the purely economically determined 'class situation' we wish to designate as status situation every typical component of the life fate of men that is determined by a specific, positive or negative, social estimation of honor," (1978, p.932). However, as previously mentioned, honor means a great deal more than social prestige, or vertical differentiation. Weber recognized horizontal as well as vertical stratification among status groups, (p.391; p.1180). More fundamentally, the social honor defining a status group is a sense of obligation among members about things one must or must not do. The following quote from Weber illustrates his use of the term honor to designate a moral code: "A sense of dignity is the precipitation in individuals of social honor and of conventional demands which a positively privileged status group raises for the deportment of its members," (p.934). Conventional demands in our terms would mean expectations with regard to acceptable behavior—normative standards. Complying with such demands is the stuff of honor. Throughout Weber's writings various terms are mentioned in the context of social honor (1946, p.88, 95, 96, 187, 189, 241, 310). Among these are: "integrity," "moral discipline," "responsibility," "discretion," "sense of dignity," "respectable," "distinguished," and above all "a specific style of life." Most particularly, honor within a group means adherence to a particular code of conduct, the style of life. Weber says, "Status is a quality of social honor or lack of it, and is in the main conditioned as well as expressed through a specific style of life," (1946, p.405). Weber adds that it is "expected from all those who wish to belong to the circle," (1978, p.932).

As previously discussed, in contemporary terms a group's style of life is the group's subculture. Bendix makes this point in the following comment about Weber's use of the concept in a particular study: "It also was necessary to analyze ideas derived from the subculture of each group—in Weber's terms, its 'style of life,'" (1977, p.85). Bendix also says in reference to style of life, "However, Weber's use of the term includes all instances of cohesive social groups with their subcultures and their exclusion of outsiders," (p.85n). The practice of excluding outsiders will be taken up in a later section of this essay. Here, one must note that the characteristics of a status group may apply to a group irrespective of its social standing. Indeed, Weber was very interested in status groups that were designated as pariahs, especially the medieval Jews. One could say that members of the American Mafia, and of many other criminal groups, exhibit a sense of honor, or *omerta*, every bit as much as a New England Yankee or a Southern Gentleman.

The term conventions, as used by Weber, has been mentioned several times in this essay. As the host of a particular subculture and a code of behavior, a status group is the carrier of social norms—in Weber's terms "conventions," (1978, pp. 935-936). In whatever way it may appear, all stylization of life either originates in status groups or is at least conserved by them. According to Swedberg, "Weber's term convention has roughly the same meaning as 'norm' in contemporary sociology; and it plays an important role in his sociology," (2005, p.53). Bendix elaborates as follows: "Weber defined convention as conduct induced 'without any direct reaction other than the expression of approval or disapproval on the part of those persons who constitute the environment of the actor,'" (1977, p.264n). That is, it is not induced by material compensation or organizational authority. Expanding upon the idea of status groups as the bearers of norms, this essay suggests that status groups are generally the bearers of conventional beliefs, and conventional values, as well as conventional notions of correct behavior. One could say that status groups have a sort of fiduciary relationship to particular beliefs, values, and norms. Whereas ideas are doubtless conceived by individuals, they will not survive the individual's mortality unless adopted by a status group. Nor will they have a general effect in society unless adopted by a group, organized or unorganized.

With regard to style of life, Weber referred to many attitudes or practices from daily life. In a contemporary context, one could refer to such characteristics as: a sense of identity, community or "we-ness;" a rationalization for the superiority of one's group; a view of outsiders as inferior in some respect; a body of esoteric knowledge or expertise; a sense of place or home territory; a cast of heroes or villains; a regard of certain documents, artifacts, etc. as sacred or very special; a code of behavior; a group story or historical narrative; a special language, argot, slang, or dialect; a preferred form of habitat; and a unique set of symbols or gestures. In addition, such elements of a status group culture may be expressed in related practices. These may include behaviors such as: unique ceremonies or rituals; socialization, initiation, or induction practices; recreation and leisure; wearing special clothes or fashionable apparel; distinctive cuisine, art, architecture, music, dance, or literature; and exclusivity or avoidance of outsiders.

A breach of conventions, or norms—hence action against group honor— can lead to shunning or expulsion from a status group. Weber declares:

> *A violation of conventional rules—such as standards of "respectability" (Standessitte)—often leads to the severe and effective sanction of an informal boycott on the part of members of one's status group. This may actually be a more severe punishment than any legal penalty. (1978, p.34)*

Weber also says violations of status conventions (i.e., norms, code of honor) can lead to an individual's "status disqualification," (1946, p.191).

In the context of a discussion of status groups, this essay will briefly consider the idea of community. In doing so, it largely agrees with Cohen's conception of community. This does not contradict Mead or Weber. As expressed in the following quotes, Cohen (1985) views community as based on shared culture, or subculture:

> *Thus, moving away from the earlier emphasis our discipline placed on structure, we approach community as a phenomenon of culture: as one, therefore, which is meaningfully constructed by people through their symbolic powers and resources. (p.38)*

> *In other words, we have to treat them as symbolic forms. (p.40)*

> *Community exists in the minds of its members, and should not be confused with geographic or sociographic assertions of fact. (1p.98)*

> *The reality of community lies in its members' perception of the vitality of its culture. (p.118)*

Cohen further elaborates:

> *The quintessential referent of community is that its members make, or believe they make, a similar sense of things either generally or with respect to specific and significant interests, and, further, that they think that that sense may differ from one made elsewhere. The reality of community in peoples experience thus inheres in their attachment or commitment to a common body of symbols. (p.16)*

> *Rather, it exists as something for people "to think with." The symbols of community provide people with the means to make meaning. (p.19)*

Weber says of community, "Communal action refers to that action which is oriented to the feeling of the actors that they belong together," (1946, p.183). Cohen (1985) agrees:

It is a matter of feeling, a matter which resides in the minds of the members themselves. Thus, although they recognize important differences among themselves, they also suppose themselves to be more like each other than like the members of other communities. (p.21)

It is, of course, a prime characteristic of status groups that the members feel in some sense that they belong together. It follows that status groups are typically a basis of community. Weber states, "In contrast to classes, status groups are normally communities," (1946, p.186). A principal characteristic of status groups is common lifestyle; which Bendix interprets as subculture, and Cohen explicitly relates subculture to community. Status group identity, a shared subculture, a sense of community—all may rise in conjunction with the extended interaction of a group's members.

Sometimes groups based on a subculture, or a distinctive style of life, are referred to as identity groups, sometimes as reference groups, sometimes as a community, but generically they are status groups. This difference in terminology is largely a matter of context. They are groups with distinctive elements of subculture and recognized social standing. This accords with Mead's views on community. For Mead, a community is based on communication and a common response to events. A community is the host of a generalized other— an organized set of attitudes by which individuals can take the attitudes of the group as a whole into their own action. Mead says, "The organized community or social group which gives to the individual his unity of self can be called 'the generalized other.' The attitude of the generalized other is the attitudes of the whole community," (1965b, p.218). Recalling the baseball illustration of a generalized other, it provides the player with a sense of position, of collegiality, of perspective on what to do, and of team identity.

A core concern, here, is the role of status groups in providing a basis for collective action in society, and in organizations. Status groups, as the bearers of subcultures, have distinctive beliefs, values, and norms. As such, they provide commitments to both means and ends of social action. The effect of status groups is frequently demonstrated in political action. Politics is concerned with the arrangement of collective means and ends— the disposition and exercise of authority. Accordingly, status group beliefs, values, and norms are often called upon to coalesce political support, or political opposition. Further, it should come as no surprise that status group distinctions, or characteristics, are frequently employed in politics as wedge issues. As wedge issues, status group convictions may be used to increase or decrease electoral participation, or to produce support or opposition for issues or candidates. In political circles, status groups are often referred to as "identity groups." As such, status groups play an important role in political disputes such as the legality of abortions, gun control legislation, prayer in public schools, gay or lesbian marriage, English as an official language, immigration policies, and racial or ethnic affirmative action. In each case the issue may be used to polarize an electorate along the lines of status group differences—or life-style markers. Of course, status groups, as generative of social action, may have analogous effects within an organization. This point was discussed earlier in this essay.

Status groups often function as reference groups. That is, attitudes that are characteristic of status group members may be consciously invoked, even by nonmembers, in addressing a particular circumstance. According to Shibutani, who wrote extensively about reference group behavior, "In this usage a reference group becomes any collectivity, real or imagined, envied or despised, whose perspective is assumed by the actor," (1955, p.563). Shibutani also says, "A reference group, then, is that group whose outlook is used by the actor as the frame of reference in the organization of his perceptual field," (p.565). Sibutani was fully aware that a reference group functions in Mead's terms as an other, or more particularly as a generalized other in reflexive action and thought (p.564). Shibutani also described reference groups in terms that may be seen as referring to status groups (p.567). He spoke of differential association, a special universe of discourse, special meanings and symbols, social distance from outsiders, norms of conduct, a set of values, a special prestige ladder, a common outlook toward life, and a code of honor. Thus one must assume that status groups, in Shibutani's perspective, commonly function as reference groups. Actually, it is quite obvious that members of a status group, which bears a subculture, will often consciously call upon the group's outlook when reflexively considering their own or other's actions. Of greater interest, here, is the notion that individuals in organizations will call upon the perspectives of various status groups, as reference groups, when addressing problems of individual or collective action. Particularly in collective action, one is likely to call upon the perspectives of established groups with relevant viewpoints. In an organization, one learns that when deliberating about a problem or an issue, it is wise to mentally review how the matter may be viewed by the several collective others, established others, who may have influential opinions. As to the conjunction of status groups and taking the attitudes or others, this will be discussed further in the next chapter.

CHAPTER X.

Party

Party, as an ideal type, may be used to analyze political contention and action based on allegiance to authority, in organizations as in societies. Organizations center upon mobilizing individuals for purposes of collective action. Exercise of authority and the quest for authority are principal means for achieving that mobilization. Thus, the authority arrangement is generally of great importance in an organization. However, one must assume there is always some struggle over the disposition and exercise of authority. Organizations are inherently political bodies. Inevitably groups arise with somewhat different agendas with respect to where authority (collective decision making) should be lodged and to what ends it should be put. For one thing, they arise because there are groups, or collectivities, whose material or ideal concerns are differently affected by the exercise of authority. Then too, there are groups that value authority, or legitimate power, in and of itself, and seek to attain it. Further, there may be groups outside an organization that seek to intervene and affect the disposition and use of organizational authority. The contention over authority in an organization may be latent or manifest. It may be open or it may be suppressed. However, a careful analyst will look for signs of a struggle over organizational authority. However inchoate or well formed, it is likely to be there in some manner. The construction and use of ideal types, or sensitizing concepts, of party will assist in the identification and analysis.

It was previously noted that status groups are the bearers of culture, or collectively held ideas, hence shared normative orientations to action. Classes are the bearers of shared interests, hence the likelihood of shared utilitive orientations to action. Parties are the bearers of collective allegiances to authority, or aspirations to authority, hence shared authoritive orientations to action.

Parties are simply groups of individuals organized to effect the disposition and use of authority. Insofar as individuals or groups participate in organized action that is directed at attaining or influencing authority, they are distributed, or spread, among parties or party-like groups. Of course, the term party, like the terms status group and class, as an ideal type may cover a broad range of examples. It is commonly recognized that parties exist in national, state, and local politics. As previously mentioned, Weber affirmed that parties may exist in "associations," or organizations, as well as in states. A state, after all, is simply one form of organization, or organized action. Recall that Weber defines a state as an organization that successfully claims a monopoly over the use of legitimate force (1978, p.54–55). As to the inevitable contention over authority in organizations, Weber implies restricting the term "political" struggle to states. He frequently uses the term "struggle for power" in other instances. However, herein, the term political is used more generally.

> Status groups are the bearers of culture, or collectively held ideas ... classes are the bearers of shared interests ... parties are the bearers of collective allegiances to authority.

It was mentioned earlier that a party—considered as an ideal type—is an organization, whereas a class in its pure form is only an aggregate, and status group in its pure form is a social group. It should not pass unnoticed, then, that the same plurality of individuals could, at once, be a class, a status group, and a party. A group of professionals, similarly educated, similarly employed, and politically organized, could, for some purposes, be one example. Physicians, nurses, or another health professional group, in a federal, state, or local government hospital, and very likely politically engaged through a union or association, are probable examples. Such a coincidence of class, status group, and party may provide unusually strong group cohesion and effective action. Perhaps one should call such an example: "a class, a class in itself, and a class for itself." A similar phrase has been erroneously attributed to Karl Marx. In any case, a proponent of organized action would surely want class, status group, and party to be synergistic. That is, the supporter of organized action would want class interests, status group values, and party allegiances to be aligned and interacting in common purpose. This is true regardless of which dimension of meaning is dominant.

Weber made it clear that parties are highly variable. They may be tightly or loosely organized. In a full expression of the ideal type, a party will tend to be tightly controlled. It is, after all, necessarily concerned with authority, or legitimate power. One can, therefore, imagine a continuum from low to high solidarity among parties. Within an association, or everyday organization, in comparison to a nation state, one may expect parties to be more informal and less highly organized. As previously mentioned, one may refer to a party, or party-like action, as a faction, a clique, a caucus, a block, or even a tendency— whichever term is appropriate. The key consideration is whether or not there is some effort to organize action that is directed at attaining or influencing authority. A point that should not be neglected is that the administrative group in an organization may itself be considered a party, or a coalition of parties. It is the party in control. For example, in the national teachers' union, later to be discussed at length, the executive council frequently concludes its periodic meetings and immediately reconvenes, as a caucus, or party, to consider organizational politics. This separation is appropriate, and it is also legally necessary.

To recap, Weber asserts, "'Parties' reside in the sphere of power… Parties are, therefore, only possible within groups that have an associational character," (p. 938). In the terms of this essay, they only exist in groups that have organized action. That is, groups that have an administration, an arrangement for making and implementing collective decisions. Party members attempt to shape organized action by focusing on the means of organized action, the collective decision making process. They seek to capture or influence the authority arrangement, or administration, of an organization. Weber says, "Parties aim precisely at influencing this staff, and if possible, to recruit from it party members," (p. 938). One may expect party action to be directed at collective decisions such as: defining the scope of decision making; selecting leaders, or decision makers; establishing collective goals and objectives; formulating an agenda for collective action; adopting strategy and tactics; requisitioning and allocating resources; promulgating policy and rules. Furthermore, the party decision making may be concerned with an exercise of authority within the host organization, or external to the host.

The substantive concerns of parties, that is the basis of appeal to supporters, reflects the organizational dimensions previously discussed. Parties appeal to supporters, and to the activist cadre, on the basis of utilitive, normative, and authoritive orientations to action. Weber (1978) says:

> *The goal may be a cause (the party may aim at realizing a program for ideal or material purposes), or the goal may be personal (sinecures, power, and from these, honor for the leader and the followers of the party. Usually the party aims at all of them simultaneously. (p.938)*

Note that even with respect to leaders and activists—the cadre of the party— there is likely to be a mix of utilitive, normative, and authoritive orientations to action. Weber refers to sinecures, power, and honor. Furthermore, the constituencies served by a party's actions to gain or influence authority—the origins of utilitive, normative, and authoritive orientations—are likely to be class-based, status group-based, and party-based. Weber states:

> *In any individual case, parties may represent interests determined through class situation or status situation and they may recruit their following from one or the other. But they need be neither; in fact they are more likely to be mixed types, and sometimes they are neither. (p.938)*

Of course, the party cadre is, itself, a constituency, as well.

In his discussion of parties, Weber identifies three types of parties: "patronage," "ideological," and "charismatic," (Swedberg, 2005, p.194). It follows that these also express an emphasis upon utilitive, normative, and authoritive orientations. The idea will not be pursued in this essay, but one may further suggest that charisma in its purest, strictly ideal type form is entirely an authoritive orientation. Said otherwise, it is an absolute delegation of collective decision making, unrestrained by rational or traditional considerations. The delegation is claimed, and it stands, on the basis of its own merits. With respect to all of the foregoing, one may also state the action of party adherents in terms of the means and ends of social action. Some adherents pursue legitimate power to attain material ends, i.e. interests. Some pursue legitimate power to achieve ideal ends, i.e., beliefs, values, norms. And, finally, some who pursue

> Charisma is the ideal type, or limiting concept, of being drawn to the means of organized action, i.e., authority.

legitimate power are drawn not to the ends, but to the means of collective action, i.e., authority, irrespective of the ends to which it may be put. Once again, charisma is the ideal type, or limiting concept, of being drawn to the means of organized action, i.e., authority.

The contention over authority in organizations—proprietary or nonprofit, public or private, large or small, and so forth—is ubiquitous. Examples of party contention within organizations include: corporate proxy fights, association leadership elections, corporate leadership successions, struggles for gender and ethnic rights, union recognition contests, and legislative battles in assemblies. Other examples may include the following, if organized: struggles among departments or divisions, struggles among central, regional, and local offices, line versus staff, and cliques among organizational personnel. A number of scholars have documented organized contention over collective decision making. Selznick's (1966) study of the TVA relates how that federal organization struggled with organizational constituents to implement a new law. Lipset, Coleman, and Trow (1962) document a highly organized two- party system within the printers' union. Gouldner (1954) studied the struggles among different groups in a gypsum factory and mine. And, Dalton (1966) examined the power struggles of various cliques and management groups in an industry.

As with class aggregates and status groups, party organizations may not be exclusive to an organization. They may extend beyond a host organization. Just as an external class situation (e.g., wage rates, benefits) may affect those similarly situated within an organization, and external status groups (e.g., ethnic, gender, professional) may affect those with similar identities within an organization, party action within an organization may be tied to party action outside of the organization. A clear example is the action of the Communist Party within American trade unions. Clearly the American Communist Party, at one time or another, controlled a number of American trade unions, and significantly influenced many others. Of course, it is true of all totalitarian parties that they seek to control or greatly influence any organizations they target as useful. One can readily see in post-USSR Russia that the Communist Party extends its control into all manner of domestic organizations.

In this discussion of class, status, and party, it may be helpful to revisit an earlier exposition. Of course, class, status group, and party are, in the first instance, ideal types. The primary consideration here is not the factual existence of class, status group, or party entities, but whether or not the concepts are useful in analysis. Class references an individual's position in the task structure (e.g., division of labor) and related exchange relations (e.g., market position). And, according to Kingsley Davis, structure refers to "what is" in social relations. Thus, one may say class references one's position in "what is" going on. Status group references an individual's position in the distribution of culture. That is, what subculture does one fit into; where does one fit in with respect to beliefs, values, and norms. According to Kingsley Davis, culture refers to "what ought to be" in social relations. Thus, status group references one's position with respect to "what ought to be" going on. Party references one's allegiance with respect to the distribution of authority, or collective decision making. By extension one could say, on behalf of Kingsley Davis, that authority, or collective decision making, references "what is becoming" in social relations. This is illustrated by the exercise of authority in planning, policy formation, budgeting, setting objectives, outlining strategy and tactics, and so forth. Thus party, in its quest for authority, the control of collective decision making, seeks to control "what is becoming," or the emerging properties of an organization. Shortly it will be apparent that these organizational forms of what is, what ought to be, and what is becoming— manifestations of class, status group, and party—are analogous to Mead's accounting of an individual's me, other, and I, respectively.

> Manifestations of class, status group, and party —are analogous to Mead's accounting of an individual's me, other, and I, respectively.

To review this essay's methodological position, it is speaking of collective action and of an abstracted individual's place in collective action. It is not saying all action within an organization fits the ideal types of class, status group, or party. Rather, these are concepts, standards, against which action— collective action—can be tested. They are analytic concepts. Again a quote from Weber: "By the terminology suggested here, we do not wish to force schematically the infinite and multifarious historical life, but simply to create concepts useful for special purposes and for orientation," (1946, p.300). Weber's ideal types and Blumer's sensitizing concepts are aids in forming an interpretative understanding of collective action. However, there is an almost irresistable tendency to concretize, to reify, the terms class, status group, and party. It is essential to understand that such terms are abstractions, simply designed to help identify and trace the different threads of action that make up a larger social fabric. As ideal types they will have only a relative, partial correspondence to any particular collective action of individuals. There is in fact no class, status group, or party in any perfected sense. There is only group action which seemingly complies to perhaps a significant extent with the idealized concepts, in respect to the prevalent orientations and patterns of action of the participants.

The rationality featured in organized action—an explicit concern with means and ends of collective action—is comparable to reflexivity in individual action. Neither Mead nor Weber would suggest that individuals are objectively rational in their behavior, but that their most selfconscious, reflexive behavior is intentionally rational. Of course, rationality is a chief concern of Weber. And, reflexivity is a chief concern of Mead. One may additionally say, as was previously suggested, that Weber's concepts of class, status group, and party may be viewed as analogous to Mead's concepts of me, other, and I. However, this is not to suggest that an organization is in any sense a super- human, selfconscious entity. Rather, with respect to groups or organized groups, one is merely speaking of abstracted qualities of collective action.

At this point it is appropriate to review Mead's exposition of individual reflexivity, or the process of individual intelligence. Reflexivity arises in the course of action needing reconstruction. The individual treats the self as an object—along with other objects—in order to problem solve. Objectifying oneself is done by symbolically standing apart, taking the attitude, or perspective, of another. The individual visualizes the self as me, the objectified self in the problematic situation, and in the course of possible actions. Upon identifying a satisfactory course of action, the action emerges in the form of I. The individual's reconstituted action is thus an emergent. The individual controls action not by selection of response, but by identifying a suitable stimulus. Read stimulus as identifying a suitable object, or an arrangement of objects, inasmuch as an object is a collapsed act.

As to the analogous part, the management, or formal leadership, within an organization typically stands somewhat apart and opposite the remainder of the organization. That is, in an organization, authority distinctions are typically "pulled out," explicitly recognized, and stand in a relationship over and against the remainder of the organization. The management's action, a part of organized action, treats the organization as an object. Management objectifies the organization, as a whole or in part, viewing it in its context, considering various possible actions, doing this especially when the situation is problematic. In so doing, the management may take the attitudes of a range of others, within or without the organization. Within the organization these may be marketing, finance, public relations, production, and so forth. These typically are professional, subcultural groups, such as would be relevant to the functioning of a complex organization. Perhaps management will consider the attitudes of competing management groups, regulatory agencies, or the general attitudes of various publics. Insofar as the attitudes assumed by management in addressing an organizational matter are those of individuals, the individuals very likely are representative or typical of particular groups. As with individual intelligent action, management's reconstitution of organizational action probably has an emergent quality. The upshot is, rationality within organized social action is comparable to reflexivity in Mead's social psychology. One may say the processes are analogous at different levels of analysis. In each case there is a process of symbolically breaking an action into components, changing or rearranging the components, and reconstructing the action in terms of means to an end.

The key function of management, or an administration, is making decisions with regard to the means and ends of action. More particularly, this amounts to responding to organizational problems and making adjustments so as to satisfactorily continue collective action. Here, one may recall Blumer's comments about the similarity of intelligent action of individuals and organizations:

> *The same sort of picture exists in the case of the social action of a collectivity, such as a business corporation, a labor union, an army, a church, a boy's gang, or a nation. The difference is that the collectivity has a directing group or individual who is empowered to assess the operating situation, to note different things that have to be dealt with, and to map out a line of action. The self-interaction of a collectivity is in the form of discussion, counseling, and debate. The collectivity is in the same position as the individual in having to cope with a situation, in having to interpret and analyze the situation, and having to construct a line of action. (1986, p.55–56)*

This may be personalized as follows: when I consider my material circumstances and my place in the structure of action, as a participant within an organization, I may be said—borrowing Weber's use of term—to be viewing myself in a class, or class-like situation. That is, generally speaking, my tasks, environmental conditions, tangible resources, patterns of interaction, material inducements, etc. constitute my class situation within the context of the organization. They constitute my interests and exchange relationships. Along with other individuals, in comparable situations in the same or other organizations, I share a class or class-like aggregate. However, from Mead's perspective, when I am looking at myself in a particular task situation, perhaps solving a problem, I am objectifying myself as me. Again, from Weber, when I consider my action from the viewpoint of relevant groups within or without the organization—such as managers, specialized staff, professional groups, organizational cliques, minority groups, etc.—I am likely using the perspectives of status groups, or status-like groups. That is, insofar as these groups have standing and distinctive ideas one is speaking generically of status, or status- like groups. And, it is the reaction, the views of such groups, or individuals who represent such groups, that I must consider when making a decision on behalf of the organization. I am not likely to assume the attitudes of groups, or individuals from groups, that do not have recognizably distinct ideas and some standing. Of course, using Mead's terms, I am taking the attitudes of others, or generalized others, towards my possible action. I am objectifying myself from the viewpoint of others. When I take action, which is organizational action, I do so presumably at the behest of management, the administration. Management, one may recall, represents the dominant party, the holder of authority, in an organization. At the same time, using Mead's terms, my taking action, with authority delegated by the management party, is an expression of I. In individual terms, it is I considering the situation of me from the perspectives of others. Again borrowing and extending the analytic distinctions of Kingsley Davis, class and me, situated in a "factual order" or objective aspect of social action, refer to "what is," status group and other, situated in a "normative order" or subjective aspect of social action, refer to "what ought to be," and party and I, situated in an authoritive, decisional order or reflexive aspect of social action, refer to "what is becoming." Altogether, one may say that class, status group, and party are analogous to me, other, and I, albeit at different levels of analysis. With respect to organized action, one set of terms addresses behavior in the context of rational collective action, the other addresses it in the context of reflexive individual action.

CHAPTER XI

Comparability

To better illustrate the correspondence of Weber's concepts, class, status group, and party, with Mead's concepts, me, other, and I, perhaps a simple example will suffice. Consider the following narrative of the author's experience lobbying for an amendment in the US Congress. This narrative comes from a time when the author was a policy analyst and lobbyist for the national teachers' union, the American Federation of Teachers. During this period, the AFT had several thousand state and local affiliate unions, and altogether had more than a million members in states and communities across the United States. Within these state and local affiliates there were usually several membership divisions. These included teachers, paraprofessionals (teacher assistants), health care (mostly nurses), state employees, and higher education (mostly professors). In addition, there were a few miscellaneous groupings, such as physicians or lawyers. Many of the union's local affiliates had large numbers of paraprofessional educators as members. This was particularly true in dense, urban areas that typically were impoverished, blighted areas. Also, a large proportion of the paraprofessionals were minority women.

Paraprofessionals make a unique and valuable contribution to public elementary and secondary education. They provide assistance to classroom teachers, allowing a better use of the teacher's time. They provide a valuable link to the school's surrounding community, in which many of them live. Being drawn from the surrounding communities, paraprofessionals give a school's students more stability, or continuity, in their daily lives. And, many paraprofessionals go on to become teachers. This is particularly the case if their union contract provides tuition benefits, released time, and such. And, bringing paraprofessionals into the teaching staff is especially valuable in urban, teacher-shortage areas. However, at this particular time, the time referenced in this narrative, many paraprofessionals had a serious and recurring problem. They were unemployed during the summer months, when school was in recess. For many this was an enormous problem. They were usually located in areas with little, or no, employment alternatives. In contrast to school paraprofessionals, many other seasonal workers were, at that time, eligible for federal unemployment compensation during non-work periods. For example, workers in construction, landscaping, tourism, farming, and entertainment industries often enjoyed such benefits. However, benefits for seasonal workers varied greatly by states, according state enabling legislation and employer resistance.

Allowing school paraprofessionals to be eligible for federal unemployment compensation could yield a number of benefits. It would likely create a more stable workforce, develop stronger school ties to the surrounding community, and improve the standard of living of many poor students. All of these are thought by many educators to have demonstrable, educational value. Accordingly, the leaders of several AFT local unions took the issue to their US Congress representatives. And, several of these representatives were discussing an amendment to the federal unemployment compensation law. The amendment would allow paraprofessionals to receive unemployment benefits during summer recess. Upon learning of this activity, I immediately undertook the task of getting greater information about the amendment and working aggressively for its passage. With respect to its passage, the most important fact about the amendment was that it did not require local school systems to provide unemployment compensation to paraprofessionals. It simply allowed them to provide, and fund, the benefit if they chose to do so. Of course, this would entail some cost and perhaps be subject to collective bargaining.

I began working on the amendment, doing all of the things that a lobbyist would ordinarily do. Early in this process it is essential to mentally work through the entire course of action. I did this by thinking about my ensuing action from the very general perspective of a lobbyist, specifically an education and labor lobbyist. From this viewpoint I imagined myself performing all of the various tasks that I knew such lobbying would demand. I mentally outlined a probable course of action, making note of alternatives possibilities along the way, objectifying myself in the sequence of the tasks I must perform, the likely reactions of various individuals, and so on. In thinking through the tasks ahead, it is particularly important to consider the legislative setting, or environment in which an issue is situated. The setting, in this case, was by and large, one of organizations that previously had shown interest in shaping education or labor legislation. There was a variety of such organizations, organizations that might have material, ideal, or political concerns with the legislation. Organizations express these concerns by adopting policies, informing and activating members, hiring lobbyists, making political endorsements, donating campaign funds, communicating in various ways with members of congress, and so forth. Thus, I had to ask myself, "What collectivities exist that by virtue of sundry interests and concerns will likely support or oppose the proposed paraprofessional amendment?" Of course, each such organization might have a number of concerns with the amendment. Not to be neglected when considering organizations are the numerous groups and organizations within the congress and the administration – parties, caucuses, committees, subcommittees, study groups, etc.

Early in my career at the AFT, I discovered the most informative way to analyze the support or opposition for any piece of legislation is by employing Max Weber's ideal types of class, status group, and party. Said otherwise, I found it highly advantageous to interpret action in terms of aggregates and groups of individuals with different material, ideal, or dominance concerns. As stated earlier in this essay, these concepts by Weber may be used to pull apart the threads that make up a social fabric, the social process. Using the concepts of class, status group, and party to disaggregate support and opposition to a simple amendment may appear to be unnecessary – conceptual overkill. Nonetheless, they can have great value, just as they may have with complex legislation such as major tax or health care bills. This is not to say that all action may be analyzed productively as class, status group or party action. Rather, the power of these terms – and the concern of this entire discussion – is with the interpretation of collective action, action of individuals in aggregates, groups, and organized groups. Accordingly, it is suggested that, in forming an interpretive understanding of complex social action, one may benefit by looking for patterns of class, status group, and party, or their similitudes. This may neglect the idiosyncratic action of one or a few individuals.

Within the context of this essay, class is a collection or aggregate of individuals who perform a common type of task and are in similar exchange relationships. The reference here is to overt patterns of action. In society at large one may distinguish, for example, plumbers, carpenters, and electricians. However, one may also distinguish those who are self-employed from those who work for various types of employers. Any such group or subgroup will likely have distinct material interests. With reference to the paraprofessional amendment, there are a number of groups that because of their common tasks and exchange relationships may have distinctive material interests. Within the educational establishment a number of such class identifications are possible, and they presumably have some difference in objective interests. In the context of public elementary and secondary education one finds school board members, school administrators, teaching staff, and ancillary staff – such as librarians, counselors, nurses, and paraprofessionals. A further important distinction is between those who are unionized and those who are not unionized – a very different economic standing.

Status groups have, to again borrow the phrase, a fiduciary relationship to a particular culture or subculture – beliefs, values, and norms – and to the related practices of expressing and sharing that culture. Such groups tend to have not only distinctive ideas, but also cohesiveness and a recognized social standing. However, in the words of Weber, status groups may be quite amorphous. In the broader society they may include ethnic, religious, regional, gender, age cohort, and many other identity groups. Weber notes, in particular, that professional groups are usually status groups. Within local school systems obvious status groups are administrators, teachers, librarians, counselors, and paraprofessionals. Each by virtue of specialized training has, to some extent, the above mentioned characteristics of a status group. These status group distinctions overlap the earlier mentioned class distinctions, however the reference here is to professional or paraprofessional culture, not to economic interests. As discussed earlier in this essay, a group can be simultaneously a class, a status group, and a party. These analytic distinctions often overlap in practice, but one may nonetheless separate them conceptually. This is because over time, class, status group, and party orientations lead to very different patterns of action. Turning to status groups outside the education establishment, there are various policy groups and organizations that seek to influence school practices. These include, for example, the many nonprofit organizations that conduct educational research. Each tends to have its own ideas about elementary and secondary public education. Whatever the disposition of status groups, I was reasonably sure that groups with strong views on the paraprofessional unemployment compensation issue surely would make these views known.

Party is, of course, related to the system of authority, or collective decision making, within an organization. It is organized action to affect the holding or exercise of authority. Said otherwise, it is coordinated action to set the course, or order, of collective action. Thus, within the country at large we have the principal parties, the Democrats and Republicans. They seek to influence the exercise of authority at all levels of government. However, as mentioned earlier, Weber noted that parties may exist in non-governmental organizations, as well. Within education institutions, unions rise to challenge the discretion, the decision-making of governing officials. This action, generally resisted by these officials, may be viewed as party action. It is action to affect the disposition and use of authority. Within congress, where the paraprofessional amendment was to be considered, there were obvious party differences on the issue. Also, public employee unions, including the teachers, generally had closer ties to the Democrats. In contrast, administrators and school board members often were closer to the Republicans. This was apparently a typical labor – management separation. Other organizations that represent public school personnel, such as the librarians or counselors, were effectively non-partisan. However, their lobbyists often had strong personal relationships with one party or the other based on prior employment in congressional offices. Altogether, my examination of class, status group, and party alignments with respect to the paraprofessional issue was a matter of who might have a dog in the fight – who might have material, ideal, or dominance concerns with the outcome. These were the collective forces, including those within the congress, I had to deal with. Such entities may serve as barriers or as resources to individual lobbyists working an amendment.

After considering organizations that might take a stand on the paraprofessional issue, I came to the following conclusions. Among those likely to oppose the amendment for economic, class-based reasons, foremost was the National School Boards Association, the NSBA. Although the unemployment program would be discretionary on their part, and require state enabling legislation, it would entail a financial cost. Most strongly supporting the amendment for financial reasons would be the affiliates of unions with paraprofessional members. Their national, parent unions would, of course, advocate on their behalf. No other organizations or groups appeared to have pecuniary interests in the paraprofessional issue. As to status group considerations, I reviewed the possible groups and organizations that might have ideological concerns with the issue. The various school management groups would probably be little concerned, perhaps indifferent to the issue, because it lay outside the realm of conventional education policy. However, a few policy and professional groups and organizations might oppose the amendment, viewing it as undercutting professionalism. These needed to be watched. On the other side, unions with paraprofessional members would strongly support the amendment, as they would see it strengthening professionalism. That is, to be professional one must be recognized and properly rewarded for work. Next, I thought about the groups and organizations that might take a position on the amendment for purely political reasons. Public sector unions would see the paraprofessional issue as a way to increase their political clout. That is, union members with strong, enduring relationships to their unions are a greater political resource. Some civil rights organizations might be drawn into supporting the amendment. Urban, paraprofessional school employees are often black or Hispanic, and they are natural constituents of the civil rights organizations. The more prosperous and stable their livelihood, the more they are a political resource. There was general support among Democrats and greater opposition among Republicans for strengthening the unemployment compensation program. And, each party recognized the implications the amendment had for strengthening or holding back union political influence. Finally, there was some possibility that organizations, such as the Chamber of Commerce, might engage on the issue if it came to their attention. It might be viewed as having political ramifications beyond public education.

Although organizations provide the context of legislative activity, it is individuals who represent the organizations and carry out their activities. It is individuals who advocate, who negotiate, who make agreements, and most importantly who establish the relations of trust essential to legislative success. Accordingly, in working for passage of the paraprofessional amendment I had to approach individuals – legislators, legislative staff, other lobbyists, organizational representatives, media personnel, local union leadership, etc. It is a different level of analysis from the previous discussion of groups and organizations. In this lobbying process I had to visualize myself as interacting with "others." I had to assume the attitudes of others in guiding my actions as a lobbyist. This was in the sense specified by Mead. It included the generalized attitudes of others such as education and labor lobbyists, leaders and members of my own organization, congressional members and staff, and perhaps specific leaders and members of the relevant education organizations. It also included specific others – those I knew well and with whom had previously worked. However, these individuals were also representative of their sponsoring organizations.

Lobbying on Capitol Hill is mostly routine activity. That is, it's the performance of routine lobbying tasks. These tasks include such things as: dropping by congressional offices, distributing letters and fact sheets, attending legislative hearings and bill markups, attending representatives' or senators' campaign-related events, and participating in conferences, rallies, or demonstrations.

However, although the activity is routine, occasionally one must be very self-aware, or reflexive. The situation calls for an adjustment in the course of action. After Mead, objectifying oneself in such activities is observing me. As mentioned, one does this from the perspective of generalized others, such as that of experienced lobbyists, the perspective of one's organization, the viewpoints of various professional groups, and so forth. Very likely one considers the relevant attitudes of specific others, perhaps individuals who are personal friends or one has worked with in the past. Nonetheless, each individual typically is representative of one or another group or organization. In this reflexivity, brought about by a disruption in one's flow of routine action, one mentally tries out alternative courses of action, different orders of action. Upon recognizing a new way forward, thus removing the cause for hesitation, action is restored. This reconstruction or readjustment of action is Mead's I. I comes forth in a new course of action. One has reflexively mapped out a different plan of action.

On the Hill, when approaching each individual, I would have in mind what I thought were the most relevant attitudes of that other, expectations about their opinions on the paraprofessional issue. Naturally, I expected their attitudes to be reflective of their sponsoring organizations. I would engage them in a conversation, in a fairly routine manner, making my typical arguments on behalf of the amendment. If their response was other than I anticipated, I would necessarily and immediately become more reflexive. I would now more consciously be standing outside of the conversation, from the perspectives of various others, evaluating how the individual was responding, reviewing their organization's probable interests, and adjusting my actions accordingly. Altogether, I would be moving in and out of a reflexive mental posture. Looking back at this activity, I must assume that other lobbyists did the same. In fact, when working together on an issue, sitting together, evaluating and planning a joint action, we did so in the manner of a collective I, others, and a collective me – one could say we, others, and us. This was done just as described by Herbert Blumer. For example, the education lobbyists who regularly worked together on budget and appropriations met each morning in the Senate Chef, a fast-food restaurant in the basement of a senate office building. We collectively identified a problem, viewed it from various perspectives, considered alternative actions that might be taken, and so on.

When I began visiting offices on the Hill, I was principally viewing the paraprofessional issue and the tasks ahead from the general perspective of a labor union lobbyist. It was, after all, a matter of employment and monetary compensation. It was from this perspective I had outlined a course of action. First, I needed to contact the committee that would be considering the amendment. Specifically, I needed to contact members, or their staff, who sat on the subcommittee with jurisdiction over unemployment compensation legislation. This was a subcommittee of the Ways and Means Committee. Now, it is difficult to get the ear of members of this committee – some would say the most powerful committee in the congress. However, I expected those members with large teacher unions in their congressional districts would be more receptive. I would probably have greater success in approaching these others. In addition, those who were Democrats would be more welcoming. This was due to their generally favorable attitudes toward the unemployment program, but also because they expected future electoral support from a teachers' union. Fortunately, the Democrats enjoyed a large majority on the subcommittee and the full committee. Altogether, I contacted six of the dozen Democrats on the subcommittee. All but one was from a large urban area with a very large teachers' union. The exception was a congressional member with whom my union had a long history working on civil rights issues. This individual was the most supportive of all.

Upon contacting subcommittee members, or their staff, I received a generally favorable response to the amendment. I also learned that apparently no other lobbyist was working the issue, except for the school board's lobbyist. As expected, the National School Boards' Association opposed the amendment – mostly due to possible costs. Undoubtedly my strongest point in arguing for the amendment was that it would not be mandatory for local school systems. School boards would only provide the benefits if they wanted to and state law allowed the benefit. Looking for allies in working the amendment, I assumed that other unions with paraprofessional members in schools would be supportive. This was the Service Employees International Union (SEIU) and the American Federation of State, County, and Municipal Employees (AFSCME). I contacted the lobbyists for these unions – lobbyists I knew very well – and as expected they were supportive of the amendment. However, they were otherwise engaged with demanding issues and did not work the paraprofessional issue. Nonetheless, I knew I could call on them if absolutely necessary. They would put aside the other tasks and join my effort if they knew it was imperative.

I assumed the education organizations, other than NSBA, would be uninformed about the issue and have no compelling attitudes with respect to it. The course of events proved my assumption about these others to be true. With regard to the NSBA, their principal lobbyist was a close friend, and I judged he would prefer not to discuss the issue. Later, I learned that, like me, he didn't want to talk about it. Each of us understood there was little the other could do to resolve the policy difference between out organizations. I approached two civil rights organizations, thinking their lobbyists would be interested in the paraprofessional issue. Clearly, the prime beneficiaries were minority women in depressed urban areas. However, they did not respond as expected, they did not act on the issue, and I saw nothing I could do with them in the available time. I kept my eyes open to see if any policy organizations took to the issue, but saw no evidence they had. I asked subcommittee staff, and they had received no communications from such organizations. I did not attempt to draw in any other policy organizations, as doing so often muddies the issue. That is, I expected it could attract all manner of unnecessary and unhelpful add-ons. Generally speaking, keeping an issue low profile also keeps the entire matter simpler and more manageable.

I periodically kept in touch with the leaders of my own local unions, whose members would be most affected by the issue. I was particularly attentive to the several local leaders who had congressional representatives on the subcommittee or full committee. As I expected, these leaders were eager to contact their representative when I asked them to do so. This, of course, had more impact on the subcommittee than any other action on the paraprofessional issue. However, a day or two before the subcommittee was scheduled to markup the bill, the chairman's staff member told me – as I regularly made contact with subcommittee staff – the chairman and some subcommittee members did not want to proceed with the amendment. I assumed this meant they didn't see it as a priority and didn't want to defend it if challenged in committee or on the House floor. At that point, I had to quickly remove myself mentally from the situation and consider my options. I could call in the other unions, but there was little time for that. I could contact the NSBA and try to work out a compromise. I could try, again, to enlist the interest of civil rights groups. Given the short time available, I saw the best course was to redouble my own efforts. I told the chairman's staff that withdrawing the amendment, at this point, was unacceptable. I said that I would immediately contact my union's local leaders to inform them of the changed attitude. I did contact these leaders and, as expected, they were very disturbed by the idea of withdrawing the amendment. I asked these leaders to be very tough with their representatives, as I knew they would want to be. The local leaders quickly contacted their representatives, and their calls had the desired effect. The amendment was added to the bill, and the bill became law. Unfortunately, I have no knowledge of how many school systems provided paraprofessionals summer unemployment benefits, or may do so today.

One may, in important respects, view Weber's class, status group, and party and Mead's me, other, and I as comparable concepts – albeit at different levels of analysis. When in the previous narrative I was going around the Hill performing routine tasks – distributing letters, picking up copies of bills, etc. – these were the typical activities of the class of lobbyists to which I belonged. That is, my activities could be viewed as the common activities of an aggregate of individuals performing such tasks and similarly employed by organizations. And, indeed, there was such an aggregate. When I mentally stood outside of myself, taking the attitudes of others to assess or reconstruct my course of action – otherwise viewed as my class actions – I was objectifying me. I was looking at myself in past, immediate past, or possible future action. Thus, both class and me refer to objectifying oneself in a task situation, with associated exchange relationships. They both refer to one's situated activity. My lobbying behavior may be seen as part of a class, in a collective reference, or as me, in an individual reference. They are the same activities, but the perspective toward them, the context in which they are viewed, is different. As said, my pattern of actions on the Hill is typical of my class, and it's me.

With respect to status groups, or status-like groups, they have distinctive ideas, some measure of cohesiveness, and a recognized standing. Also previously stated, Weber observed that professional groups are generally status groups. In the above narrative, the groups and organizations I called upon as generalized others, or the individuals representing them I used as specific others, were generally professional groups, or individuals from professional groups. If not status groups per se, they were status-like groups. One may also recall that Weber said status groups are often amorphous. Further, it is unlikely I would have called upon a group, or an individual from a group, if the group did not have a distinctive perspective, cohesion, and recognized standing. Otherwise, why would I have thought the group's attitudes were relevant to the ongoing action? Now, status group and other, both offer prescriptions for social action. Speaking more broadly, one may say that status groups are principal bearers of generalized others. The preceding narrative identifies professional groups as status groups, and professional groups are easy to observe. This makes the correspondence fairly obvious. In a different example, the correspondence might be equally valid but less apparent. In any case, the value of correspondence is whether or not it contributes to analysis and an interpretative understanding.

In the narrative of lobbying, my actions as I were part of a collective party action. For example, I acted in concert with local union leaders and with particular members of the subcommittee to achieve a legislative outcome. Additionally, party action came through in reflexive action, also action of I, to construct or reconstruct a course of action. Specifically this was the action, collectively and individually, to spur consideration of the amendment. Both party and I assert an order, an ensuing course of action. Both are directed to arranging action. Party and I, both are action upon action – a dominance relationship. Here one may recall Mead's comments about a later, consummatory action controlling prior action. So, party emerges, as does I, in reflexive, course adjusting, order-setting action responding to a need, or purported need, for the guidance of action. In an earlier example, the education lobbyists regularly met in a senate restaurant. They worked together on budget and appropriations for federal education programs. When they sat down together to determine their next activities, together it was party, but for each it was I. Then they carried out the set course of activities in a fairly routine manner. This is not to say that all individual action should be treated as class, status group, or party action. Rather, this discussion is focused on collective action, specifically ideal types, in which individual exceptions are neglected. The aim is to identify patterns that contribute to an interpretive understanding of action. This is interpretive understanding at the collective level in terms of class, status group, and party; interpretive understanding at the individual level in terms of me, other, and I. At the end, it's a question of whether or not the concepts are useful in forming an interpretive understanding.

It should not pass unnoticed that the two levels of analysis discussed in the foregoing example of correspondence may also be viewed in terms of structure and agency. When one speaks of structure this might include such things as a society's government, economy, religious institutions, education institutions, the military, and so on. These are major patterns of activity in a society. Earlier, this essay dealt with structure as the patterned activity of individuals in aggregates, groups, and organizations. Certainly the societal entities mentioned above are that. In addition, the groups and organizations that framed action on the paraprofessional amendment may be seen as structure, or structural in nature. The assemblage of groups and organizations, including those in the congress, provided the resources, the challenges, the limits, and the opportunities for passage of the paraprofessional amendment. They were enduring, widespread forms of collective action, a context that shaped the behavior of individuals. At this level of analysis the concepts of Weber are most useful. In contrast, when discussing how individuals interacted and carried out lobbying on the paraprofessional issue one may use the term agency. The individuals acting on behalf of their organizations, particularly as they reflexively made adjustments in the course of their action, were clearly demonstrating agency. The emergent patterns of action flowing from such adjustments served to reconstruct, to set a new order, to reinvent action. Emergent action breaks through constraints and ultimately produces a new pattern, a new structure of action. At this level of analysis the concepts of Mead are most useful.

CHAPTER XII

Contention

Before examining a particular example of contention within an organization, it is useful to review some of the previously touched-upon thoughts about contention. Weber largely agreed with Marx on the ubiquity of class struggle, but he added the contention of status groups and political parties. That is, he added the struggle over ideal interests and the struggle over legitimate power, or authority, to the struggle over material interests. This occurs in organizations as well as in states. The struggle may involve any imaginable mix of these collectivities and their particular orientations to action. There is an ever-present contention over economic, social or cultural, and political or authority outcomes of collective action. The struggle may be manifest, or latent; the contending collectivities may be amorphous or well-defined; the struggle may be open or suppressed; there may or may not be institutionalized arenas of struggle. The struggle may cement or divide collective action. However, it is in the nature of economic classes, status groups, and parties—the contenders in this struggle—to produce assertive action. For example, one may choose almost any major issue under consideration in the U.S. Congress, or for that matter any state assembly, and see this interaction play out. Even on an

> It is in the nature of economic classes, status groups, and parties—the contenders in this struggle—to produce assertive action.

issue such as tax reform one will observe not only economic interests, but cultural ideas and political motives at work. The economic concerns are obvious. The moral concerns surface with issues such as whether or not to allow tax- free status for nonprofit organizations that constrain the life-style choices of clients. This includes such things as refusing to provide birth control services, or mandating abortion clients first receive anti-abortion counseling. As to political concerns, an example would be one party blocking another party's tax reform plan, to prevent that party from improving its electoral support. The continuing struggle within organizations may involve classes or class-like aggregates, status or status-like groups, and parties or party-like factions, splinter or opposition groups, etc. Such struggles occur within national corporations, within local school systems, within civic organizations, and other organizations of every kind. The primary nature of the power struggle will likely vary depending upon the ideal type of organization. That is, whether it is first and foremost a struggle over utilitive, normative, or authoritive concerns. However, interests, ideas, and authority may be to some extent "fungible." The pursuit of one may simply be a means to acquire another, and struggles may employ a range of deceptive tactics. Accordingly, one must look for a pattern of activities over a spread of time to discern the most probable objective, or meaning of the action. This may be done with ideal types, each of which implies a particular pattern or course of action. One may view a specific struggle as the contention over what an organization is becoming.

Any organization is in a continuous process of reconstruction. What appears to exist at the moment is simply a present accommodation, a "negotiated order," in the organizational narrative. With respect to the influence of outside, environmental forces, this essay earlier proposed a corollary to W. I. Thomas's famous dictum that something defined as real will be real in its consequences (1928, p.572). That is, one may say that which is not defined as real is not likely to be real in its consequences. All external forces must run the gamut of an internal struggle among classes, status groups, and parties. Indeed, it is probably by the agency of internal collectivities that external forces are represented in an organization. Finally, the perspective outlined here meets the criteria put forward by Perrow concerning a conflict view of organizations: "Theory should see conflict as an inevitable part of

> One may view a specific struggle as the contention over what an organization is becoming.

organizational life stemming from organizational characteristics rather than the characteristics of individuals," (1986, p.132).

Discussion now turns to considering an illustrative example, a case study of the contention among several highly organized caucuses—ultimately full-blown parties—in the American Federation of Teachers from the mid-1930s to the mid-1970s (Morris, 1977). This case illustrates the continuing struggle within organizations over the predominant meaning of action. From the time of its founding in 1916, the AFT experienced contention between a group of conservative local unions and a group of liberal local unions. Of course, few union teachers were truly conservative in conventional terms, and the liberal group contained many democratic socialists. This contest was not highly organized until the effects of a Communist insurgency were felt in the mid- 1930s. The Communist Party, under Moscow's direction, abandoned the attempt to foster "dual," rival unions and undertook insurgency within established unions. Within the AFT, Communist groups took control of the New York City and Philadelphia locals, a number of lesser locals, and also established many bogus locals. By making deals with conservative locals, the Communists group assumed effective control of the AFT from 1936 through 1939. The liberal group was largely removed from national offices and the executive council during this period. As the Communists were highly organized and centrally controlled, this gradually induced the liberal group, soon known as the Progressive Caucus, to also become increasingly organized.

The critical moment came at the 1939 convention, when the groups participating in the Progressive Caucus, agreed for the first time to be bound by caucus majority decisions. So, by 1939, both sides of the AFT power struggle were highly organized; they had openly adopted the normal characteristics of political parties—slates of candidates, policy platforms, and planned, disciplined convention activities. Initially their activities were confined to the annual conventions, but now they were year-round. The Communist- led group was soundly defeated in the 1940 convention, largely due to the defection of conservative locals and the increasingly obvious duplicity of the Communist group. Initially attracted to the Communist-led group by practical considerations, e.g., trading electoral support, the conservative locals found that Communist propaganda was making its way to their local members and proving troublesome. Furthermore, delegates from a number of liberal locals, who had been attracted by the Communists' high sounding rhetoric, were shocked by the Communist group's unprincipled changes in policy—dictated by the American Communist Party. With declining support from conservative locals, and with increasing general awareness of what they had been up to, the Communists were stripped of power, and several Communist locals were expelled or disbanded.

In the aftermath of World War Two, during which AFT politics had been suspended, the major AFT locals resolved into two highly organized caucuses, or political parties—the liberal Progressive Caucus and the conservative National (or Classroom Teachers') Caucus. The policy and political divisions returned to pretty much what they had been before the Communist insurgency. However, the Communist insurgency continued to bedevil the AFT, as the Communists sought to take over locals, foment convention opposition, and so on. Generally they functioned by promoting and controlling naïve candidates and by championing good-sounding issues. From post-World War Two until the mid-1960s, the Progressive and National caucuses contended for control of the AFT and disputed a number of policies. The Progressive Caucus wanted to create a greater national presence for the AFT. This involved moving the national office from Chicago to Washington, D.C., producing impressive publications, sponsoring an ambitious national organizing program, and participating in the national debate over major public issues. It included, for example, support for the United Nations, and support for federal aid to education. Most importantly, the Progressive Caucus wanted to play a role in the civil rights struggle. The AFT did submit an amicus brief to the Brown vs. Board of Education, US Supreme Court case. In addition, virtually all of the Progressive Caucus leaders during this period were extensively involved in civil rights activities. Somewhat later, they were a key part of the behind-the- scenes group organizing the March on Washington. However, the AFT had a handful of racially segregated locals, inherited from the union's very early days. The Progressive Caucus was relentless in pushing for their expulsion. This controversy, in fact, dated from the mid-1930s. The issue finally came to a head in the mid-1950s, ending the decades-old struggle, when several locals were expelled or voluntarily left the AFT. The National Caucus locals, for their part, were opposed to segregation, but wanted to take a pragmatic, gradual approach to ending segregated locals. They feared that mandating integration of the AFT's few southern locals would isolate them in their communities and ultimately destroy these locals. And, of course, it did; it destroyed the AFT's southern flank. On civil rights and other issues the National Caucus had a local focus: bread and butter unionism, support for local schools, close ties with the local labor movement, generally positive relations with the local political establishment, and a strong belief in locally-originated union organizing programs.

In the early 1960s, up-and-coming leadership in the Progressive Caucus's principal local, New York City, brashly pushed for a collective bargaining election. They succeeded, and in short order created the largest union local in the US—setting off a national wave of teacher strikes and organizing campaigns. Organizing and collective bargaining spread like a great wave throughout public education. It also created a need for a new type of AFT local union. The National Caucus locals had previously been moderate in their policies and accommodating with local school and political authorities. They scrupulously avoided divisive issues. The Progressive Caucus locals, on the other hand, were immoderate and contentious. They heartily embraced controversial issues. The new order of the day was to meld these different approaches. In short, collective bargaining locals had to be practical in terms of teacher employment issues and local labor and political relationships. They had to embrace foremost the issues that affected students and teachers' daily lives. Yet, they had to be willing to be very contentious, as in protests and strikes. Further, with a massive growth in membership, the national AFT now had the resources to sponsor widespread organizing campaigns, to back-up militant locals, and to participate meaningfully in national issue debates. The AFT had the financial resources and membership numbers to play a significant role in politics, a matter of great satisfaction to both caucuses. Thus, with the advent of teacher collective bargaining in the early 1960s, the opposition between the conservative and liberal caucuses began to dissolve. The result was a merger of the two caucuses under the banner of the Progressive Caucus, a shared leadership, and further acceleration of the AFT's growth and power. In short order, the AFT became one of the largest unions in the national federation, the AFL–CIO. Thereafter, within conventions, the merged Progressive Caucus was regularly opposed by a small, continuously changing and reemerging caucus, composed of various dissident groups. In this ever-morphing opposition caucus, old-line Communists pulled strings from behind a curtain of anonymity. (In this matter, the author's information is based on personal observation and a very significant number of interviews with all participating groups.) In the overview of AFT caucuses it is apparent there were, for the most part, three organized groups, extending over the covered time, that account for the internal power struggle. Each of the three had, at one time or another, dominant influence in the caucus system and governance of the AFT. In relative terms there was a conservative group led by the Chicago local, a progressive group generally led by the New York City local, and a continually reemerging radical group led, or orchestrated, by Communists from dissident locals. As with all parties, there was a continuing circulation of leaders, of local affiliates, and individual members. Nonetheless, there was an identifiable continuity of organized action, of bases of support, of political program. Although termed "caucuses," these groups, following 1939, had the general characteristics of political parties: a slate of candidates, a policy platform, organized convention activities, and so forth. In particular, as previously said, each caucus had adopted procedures for binding, collective decision making. This change was not easily agreed to, and it was viewed by caucus members as having great significance. In all important respects, the AFT had a robust party system. The question arises, then, how is one to explain the AFT caucuses, the continuing contest of organized parties? Interviews with a large number of caucus leaders, from all periods of the caucus history, and from each of the three caucus groups, gave rise to several possible explanations. Each explanation was carefully evaluated by the author.

A number of interviewees mentioned that in some geographical areas there were separate men's locals and women's locals, with the women's local usually being more progressive. In fact, there were separate locals for a brief time in at least two major cities. However, convention data concerning the caucuses and the major locals does not support this idea. Another idea occasionally mentioned was that the liberal caucus had a larger percentage of higher education members. The Communists did organize a number of higher education "paper" locals, and the Progressive Caucus was greatly influenced by a select group of higher education figures, but overall this idea is not at all supported by membership data. An idea, mentioned several times, was that caucus opposition was often fed by local rivalries of geographically adjacent locals. This appears to have been true in a few cases, but characteristically the opposite was true. More frequently geographic proximity was associated with political alliance. Perhaps the most popular idea was that the caucus alignment was based on regional differences in political attitudes. That is, individuals from the American Midwest were typically more conservative politically than those from the East Coast. As plausible as this idea may be, with respect to AFT caucuses it does not hold up. Among the major locals in the liberal Progressive Caucus one finds Detroit, St. Louis, West Suburban Chicago, St. Paul, and Chattanooga. And, from time-to-time (given the failure rate of locals), major locals on the East Coast or West Coast were part of the conservative National Caucus. A popular idea was that locals in the conservative caucus benefited from greater support by other unions in their home areas. It is likely that prior to the AFL–CIO merger, the conservative locals had better relations with the AFL, and the liberal locals had better relations with the CIO. However, major AFT locals typically were located in strong union areas, regardless of their caucus affiliation, and benefited from support by their local labor federations.

The author of this study searched in vain for any significant differences among the caucus locals, such as characteristics of the employing school system, prevalent type of employment of members, and so on. Ultimately, one promising lead came out of the several hundred interviews, the examination of numerous archives, the reading of four decades of convention and executive council minutes, and an extensive array of other historical records. In a handful of interviews, perhaps five or six, the interviewees stated in various ways that the locals in the National Caucus were somehow more successful that those in the Progressive Caucus. And, upon revisiting written materials, here and there were a few, similar comments. However, the Progressive Caucus and the National Caucus had a similar number of large locals, viewed in terms of membership numbers. Furthermore, none of the major locals in either caucus had achieved such milestones of union success as becoming the legal representative of a group of teachers, negotiating a collective bargaining contract, establishing procedures for contract administration, conducting a successful strike, or other measures of union strength. It is true that, later on, a number of locals claimed to have done such things, but this was a romantic retelling of teacher union history.

To understand the basis of the AFT caucus system, one must turn to an interpretative understanding of the AFT caucus activities. That is, one must examine more thoroughly, utilizing sensitizing concepts, the orientations to action prevalent among individuals in each of the different caucuses. What were their objectives? Said otherwise, what meaning did they ascribe to their union activity? And, what associated patterns of action did they exhibit? This complies with Weber's statement, "the specific task of sociological analysis or that of the other sciences of action, which is the interpretation of action in terms of its subjective meaning," (1978, p.8). More particularly, the sensitizing concepts, or ideal types, relevant here are those of class, status group, and party. Weber indicated that parties may represent class or class-like, status group or status-group-like, and party or party-like concerns. Thus, the question becomes: with these sensitizing concepts in mind, and reviewing the characteristics of each of the AFT caucuses, did each caucus clearly represent a particular orientation or combination of such orientations? And, one is reminded that interest is not in class, status group, and party as concrete, objective entities. Rather, they are heuristic concepts for identifying and pulling apart the meanings of action. Thus, the task is to interpret action in terms of its subjective meaning—to assess the extent and the manner that the AFT caucuses were the bearers of class, status group, and party expressions of meaning. Fortunately, the class, status group, and party orientations in this case, the example of the AFT caucuses, are remarkably clear and unentangled.

Class, as previously defined, is an aggregate of individuals in the same or similar task positions and associated exchange relations. As such, they have common objective, material—one may say economic—interests. Now, the mid-to-late 1930s was a particularly difficult time for public school teachers. Many of them experienced declining income, economic insecurity, and even job loss. A number of the leading locals in the AFT's National Caucus were especially concerned with these issues and were, in fact, organized or reorganized during this period. The Chicago local, the presumptive leader of the National Caucus is a good example. It was formed by a merger of four separate Chicago locals in 1936. (Said otherwise, status group distinctions among the Chicago teachers were submerged, and they were organized by class.) The leaders of the Chicago local also led a series of successful protest activities against financial corruption by Chicago officials and banks that had targeted public school teachers. According to informants for the author's study, the city withheld teacher salaries, or paid teacher in script, ostensibly due to lack of tax revenue. The teachers could exchange their script at Chicago banks, albeit at a substantial loss, and the banks used the script at full value to pay overdue city taxes. The Chicago teacher union leaders organized a series of successful protests against this corruption. They were assisted in this and other battles by the Chicago central labor body, a national AFL affiliate. This increased the bond the teachers had with the AFL local unions. The value of the bond was demonstrated very shortly after the local merger, when two teachers were fired for attempting to organize a suburban teachers' union. After nearly a year's effort by the Chicago urban local to get them reinstated, the matter was quickly resolved when the Teamsters' Union summarily shut down winter deliveries of heating coal for the suburban school authorities.

What were the primary characteristics of the Chicago local, the premier local of the National Caucus? Looking at the Chicago local, it had a very pragmatic, or practical, view of union action. For this it was repeatedly criticized by the Progressive Caucus locals. An example, previously mentioned, was the Chicago local's stand on AFT segregated locals. Chicago and the other locals in the National Caucus opposed racial segregation, but in this as in many other matters, they favored a gradualist approach. They asserted that moving precipitously would simply destroy the few segregated locals. And, they asserted that the white locals often helped the non-white locals in dealing with white authorities. Of course, there was no feasible, gradualist remedy, and the AFT simply lost all of its southern locals. As its primary concern, the Chicago local sought to improve the quality of Chicago schools and the employment conditions of Chicago teachers. It was described by some members as a "bread and butter union." The local had little interest in ideological disputes and was not particularly interested in "big ideas." Recall that for a time its leaders, in their convention activities, were untroubled in making political deals with the Communist faction.

The Chicago local's activities on behalf of teachers were primarily directed toward local authorities, the school board and city hall, who employed the teachers. This is a characteristic that Weber associates with class. Weber (1978) contends:

> *If classes, as such, are not groups, nevertheless class situations emerge only on the basis of social action. However, social action that brings forth class situations is not basically action among members of the identical class. It is action among members of different classes. (p.930)*

> *Since it is quite a general phenomenon we must mention here that the class antagonisms that are conditioned through the market situations are usually most bitter between those who actually and directly participate as opponents in price wars. (p.931)*

The principal alliances made by the Chicago local were with Chicago organizations—local unions and the local Democratic machine. Like the local AFL craft unions that it consciously emulated, the Chicago local sought to represent workers in a common task and market situation. Also, based on their experience, the Chicago local's leaders and members saw the AFL federation's unions as their most reliable supporters. Indeed, it was AFL union members' children that attended the local public schools. As to the local Democratic machine, the Chicago local's leaders were quite proud of their alliance over many years. The Chicago local's approach to union organizing also had a "close to home" focus. The Chicago leaders were very reluctant to endorse broadly ambitious AFT organizing programs. They believed that successful teacher union organizing must emanate from those most affected and most familiar with the actual employment situation.

The Chicago local sought to include in its membership all regular teachers in the public school district. This was evident in the 1936 merger that brought all Chicago public school teachers together in one local union. Said otherwise, the Chicago local, like other leading locals in the National Caucus, embraced all teachers in the same task and market situation. That is, virtually all of the local's members were classroom teachers in the Chicago public schools. Clearly, as the term is used in this essay, the Chicago local, and the National Caucus that it typified, addressed the class situation of their members. AFT members, insofar as one references their common material circumstances as school teachers employed in local public school systems, may be said to constitute a class. Accordingly, one can say that the National Caucus locals in the AFT had primarily a class orientation to union action. This was clearly evident in their action at AFT conventions, as elsewhere. The Chicago and National Caucus agenda for the AFT, an agenda that they pursued for decades, was to advocate for the class interests of public school teachers.

A status group, one may recall, is a social group with a distinctive culture—what Weber called a "style of life," or a distinctive set of "conventions," i.e., social norms. There is an outside recognition of the group's identity, with some sense of social position. The group tends to have some form of "closure," or exclusion of nonconformists. There are numerous other characteristics, as well, based on the group's commitment to particular beliefs, values, and norms. These criteria relate well to the New York City local of the AFT, as it was before and after the Communist insurgency, and as the premier local and exemplar of the Progressive Caucus. The New York City local and other major locals in the Progressive Caucus were the bearers of a distinctive professional ethos, or subculture, within American education. This distinctive ethos was an off-shoot of Progressive Education. Progressive Education was a major influence in early Twentieth Century American education. Featuring a "child- centered" approach to instruction, its leading proponent was John Dewey, the eminent pragmatist philosopher. A derivative of Progressive Education, Social Reconstructionism, became popular during the years of the Great Depression. According to Hawley (2016), "The political and economic climate of the Great Depression fueled questions about the relationships between democracy, equality, capitalism, and education in American Society." The advocates of Social Reconstructionism argued that American education should center upon progressive social reform. An impetus for social reform should be built into all aspects of the school curriculum. Bieger (2015) explains:

> *Originally led by George Counts… and Charles Rugg, a sector of the progressivists decided that a child-centered approach had to be superseded with a social approach to education wherein*

> *the schools become a force not just for individual development,*
> *but also for social change. (p.3–4)*

Reconsructionism had a very significant effect on the AFT, particularly on the Progressive Caucus. Berube concludes, "The AFT was heavily influenced by the Progressive educators at Teachers College such as Dewey and Counts with its promotion of the school as an instrument for 'social reconstruction' of American society," (2004, p.15). The leading spokespersons within AFT for Social Reconstructionism, aside from some support from Dewey, included George Counts and John Childs. All were professors at Columbia University in New York City. In addition to arguing that schools should promote progressive social reform, they were strong supporters of teacher unionism. They saw unions, in general and teacher unions in particular, as progressive social forces. Dewey, Counts, and Childs were key participants in the AFT of their time. Dewey reportedly held membership card number one in the non-Communist New York City local. George Counts was a leader of the AFT Progressive Caucus during the late 1930s and early 1940s defeat of the Communist faction. He was elected AFT president in 1939 and 1940. John Childs was an activist in the AFT at various times, from the late 1930s to the early 1950s. He served on the AFT executive council and was a leader in the Progressive Caucus. Dewey, Counts, and Childs all wrote articles for the Social Reconstructionist journal, The Social Frontier. In its first issue, the Social Frontier was described as a "prime medium for the development of constructive social consciousness among educational workers," (Murrow, 2011) Thus it follows that the leading locals of the Progressive Caucus were greatly influenced by the ideas of the Social Reconstructionists. Several of the leading Social Reconstructionists were also prominent leaders in the AFT's Progressive Caucus.

As the New York City local, before and after the Communist insurgency, was the premier local, the leading local in the Progressive Caucus, what were its defining characteristics? The New York City local appears to have been more interested in educational and social reform than teacher employment conditions. In its various activities it was focused primarily on public issues at the community, state, and national levels. Under the New York City local's guidance, the AFT Progressive Caucus wanted to establish a national presence—place the national office and a full-time legislative representative in Washington, DC, promote federal aid to education, publish a nationally recognized journal, and participate in the national dialogue on social issues. The preferred approach to union organizing was to launch a national program. With regard to its relationship with the AFL, the New York City local—and with it the Progressive Caucus—had a somewhat troubled past. On several occasions it had openly opposed the AFL policies and leadership. Many of the leading personnel in the New York City local were also active in the New York Liberal Party, the Socialist Party, and major reform organizations. Such alliances were also characteristic of many other Progressive Caucus leaders. Most important, in contrast to the Chicago Local and other locals in the National Caucus, the Progressive Caucus locals were not generally the de facto representatives of teachers in their school systems and local communities.

Of central importance here, the New York City local did not seek to organize all teachers in the local school system. The local had a very selective membership policy and was very careful about who was invited to join. No doubt this was, in part, due to the influence of Dewey, Counts, and Childs. Dewey and the Social Reconstructionists realized that only a select group of teachers would respond to their message. According to Murrow, "Dewey described teachers as lethargic and timid and in need of direction," (2011, p.316). Murrow quotes Dewey as follows:

> *In spite of the lethargy and timidity of all too many teachers, I believe there are enough teachers who will respond to the great task of making schools active and militant participants in [the] creation of a new social order, provided they are shown not merely the general end in view but also the means of its accomplishment. (p.316)*

Nearly all of the major locals in the Progressive Caucus followed the New York City local's lead in organizing only a small percentage of teachers in their school districts. Looking at membership data from the mid-1940s to the mid-1950s, with the exception of the St. Paul local, none of the major Progressive Caucus locals organized more that twenty-nine percent of their jurisdiction. The average of all of the leading Progressive Caucus locals over this period ranged from twelve to fourteen percent. In contrast, each of the major locals in the National Caucus, following Chicago's lead, became a majority organization within a year or two of formation. Before the caucus system fully emerged in 1939–1940, all of the principal locals in the Chicago-led faction had achieved majority, or near majority, standing in their jurisdictions.

In addition to embracing issues that divided teachers, and likely alienated potential members, there is clear evidence that leaders of a number of Progressive Caucus locals deliberately kept their locals minority organizations. They were concerned that too large a membership would dilute their reformist zeal. In his study of the New York City local, Cole points out that before the 1960s the local was more of a debating society than a union (1969, p.208). Similarly, in a study of the Philadelphia local, Grosser states, "Its small membership enabled it to act as the conscience of the school system," (1968, p.209). This practice of purposely limiting membership contrasted strongly with the Chicago local and the National Caucus. Locals in the National Caucus could not be majority organizations—and therefore effective as regular unions—without including some members who were, in comparative terms, moderate or conservative in their views. On the other hand, the New York City local, and other major locals in the Progressive Caucus, had what can reasonably be described as an elitist view of teacher union membership. Selectivity of membership became a very contentious issue within the New York City local in the 1960s, when a group of young activists sought to aggressively expand membership. This occurred shortly before the New York City local brashly, and effectively, launched a campaign to become the collective bargaining agent for all city teachers. Initially, the young activists were rudely rebuffed by the old guard. A leader of the older group said with respect to member applicants, "We know where we stand on issues of civil rights and civil liberties and separation of church and state, where do they stand?" (Kahlenberg, 2007, p.45).

As cited earlier, Weber viewed the development of exclusionary practices, i.e., withholding membership, as a clear sign of status group orientation. Weber stated:

> *In content, status honor is normally expressed by the fact that above all else a specific style of life is expected from all those who wish to belong to the circle. Linked with this expectation are restrictions on social intercourse (That is, intercourse which is not subservient to economic or any other purpose)... Whenever this is not a mere individual and socially irrelevant imitation of another life style, but consensual action of this closing character, the status development is underway. (1978, p.932)*

Thus, selectivity in membership, and exclusion of those who do not share important elements of the Social Reconstructionist subculture, i.e., beliefs, values, norms, is an important status group characteristic. The Social Reconstructionists in the AFT were, in the main, a professional group, and it was noted earlier that professional groups are typically status groups. Thus, it may be said that the Progressive Caucus of the AFT had primarily a status group orientation, namely that of a select group of teachers with a Reconstructionist ethos. The

Progressive Caucus locals were bound together by a common set of ideas, viewed themselves as an elite among teachers, and believed that the AFT had a reformist mission within American public education and American society. As an aside, this conclusion brings to light the fact that professionals, as mentioned earlier, may have both class and status group orientations, and these may be pulling them in different directions. The competition between the National Caucus and the Progressive Caucus exhibits this tension within a professional occupation.

The Communist Party began the 1930s instructing its labor activists to set up dual unions. That is, they were instructed to establish unions competing directly with mainstream American unions. However, by 1935, this strategy was abandoned. Communists activists were then directed to participate within mainstream unions, strive to attain power, and bend those unions toward support of the Soviet Union, its policies, and its "front" organizations. The AFT was a particular target of Communist activists, and its vulnerabilities were quickly exploited. Operating in a highly regimented manner, the Communists used disruptive tactics, undemocratic procedures, bogus membership roles, any convenient issue, unprincipled alliances, and similar tactics to gain power. One of the colorful terms used by their AFT opponents was "iron-assing," in which the Communists participating in a meeting would use stalling tactics, outlast their opponents, wait until the teachers who had regular jobs had to leave to get some sleep, and then take control and pass pro-Soviet measures. The Communist group quickly assumed control of the New York City local, the Philadelphia local, and a number of other locals. However, within a half-dozen years, chilling events such as the 1939 Hitler-Stalin Pact and the 1940 murder of Leon Trotsky, as well as the Communists' brazen activities in the AFT, caught up with them.

The Chicago-led locals and the remnant of locals formerly led by the New York City non-Communists temporarily put aside their differences. In response to the Communists' disciplined activity, the newly formed Progressive Caucus also became highly organized. Participants in the Progressive Caucus, as mentioned earlier, said the defining moment was when they agreed to democratically reach and then be bound by collective decisions. They announced the agreement at the beginning of caucus meetings, and anyone who wouldn't agree had to immediately leave. As a result of this newly-found discipline, the Communist-led caucus was thoroughly defeated. George Counts, the leading Educational Reconstructionist of the time and principal figure in the Progressive Caucus was, over the Chicago-led group's temporary objections, put forward as the Progressive Caucus presidential candidate. He served as AFT president from late 1939 through 1942. By 1941 the Communist group had been thoroughly routed. Ultimately, several Communist-dominated locals were expelled or simply fell away. New locals were chartered by the AFT in New York City and Philadelphia. Nonetheless, Communist-led groups continued in ensuing years—in the author's personal knowledge until the mid 1970s—to form opposition party actions challenging the AFT incumbent leadership. When the Progressive Caucus and the formerly National Caucus merged in the mid 1960s, the Communist faction again appeared within a dissident caucus. Thus, although open activities emerged, submerged, and reemerged, they were doubtless continuous in their activity. The author observed as late as the 1970s that key leadership of the dissident caucus came from long-term Communist Party activists. As opposed to a pragmatic orientation to class interests, or a principled orientation to status group ideas, the Communist group was thoroughly opportunistic—using any issue, any method, to gain power. It is not too much to say that the Communist faction sought only to promote the political interests of the Soviet Union and the American Communist Party. With respect to union membership, the Communist group did not channel its organizing activities to public school teachers, herein described as a class, nor to a professional elite of public school teachers, herein described as a status group. As far as union organizing was concerned, the Communist group sought to penetrate existing AFT locals, or set up new, often paper locals, and extend membership to ersatz teachers in Communist influenced organizations. The Communist leaders organized anybody they thought they could use to gain power. At the same time, inclusion in the secret Communist "cell," the inner conspiratorial group, was carefully controlled and very limited. The principal alliances of the AFT's Communist group were "front" groups of the American Communist Party. Ultimately, books written by leading Communist activists in the AFT, or their testimony before the US Congress, extensively documented their union activity. The AFT's communist group was a highly disciplined group, tightly controlled and directed from above by the American Communist Party. In their AFT convention activities they were extraordinarily well disciplined. The participants in the Progressive Caucus said they had not previously witnessed such discipline in a convention. Here, one is reminded of Weber's statement, "Since a party always struggles for political control (Herschaft), its organization too is frequently strict and 'authoritarian,'" (1978, p.939). Clearly, the Communist group had a party orientation to caucus activities. As an appendage of the American Communist Party, the Communist group in the AFT constituted an organization seeking authority within a host organization. Again, in Weber's words, "Parties reside in the sphere of power. Their action is oriented toward the acquisition of social power, that is to say, toward influencing social action no matter what its content may be," (p.938).

As to issue content, the Communist group was indiscriminate, so long as it contributed to gaining power and serving the Soviet Union.

As previously stated, the advent of widespread collective bargaining for public school teachers in the 1960s brought the AFT tremendous growth in membership numbers, in financial resources, and in political influence. The great success starting in New York City, and rapidly expanding to other major metropolitan areas, undercut the longstanding differences between the AFT's Progressive Caucus and National Caucus. Much of the debate that had separated the two caucuses was now moot. The differences between the two major caucuses subsided as a new model of teacher unionism emerged. One could say that the changes brought about by the 1960s advent of teacher collective bargaining resulted in an accommodation of the class, status group, and party orientations within the AFT. The result was a very strong and resilient organization. However, as the AFT is a union, there is little doubt that the utilitive type of orientation is dominant among members and leaders.

It has been suggested that one may think of parties as oriented to "what is becoming" in a host organization. With this in mind, the caucus contention within the AFT may be seen as principally about what kind of union it would become, where it was going, what type of meaning would prevail. It was a struggle over the various utilitive, normative, and authoritive orientations to action, and which would be dominant. The three party groups attributed different meaning to their teacher union activity—they had different objectives in mind. Although the Communist group was routed, and the Progressive Caucus became a merged caucus, the struggle was far from over. New circumstances, new challenges, brought and will bring renewed struggle. Looking back on the contention between the caucuses, it shows the ambivalence of organized professionals—when to act as a class, a status group, or a party? This ambiguity would probably also be true of organized physicians, nurses, attorneys, and other professional groups. Also demonstrated in the AFT caucus narrative, Weber made an observation that parties typically rest on three different bases of support—class, status group, and party cadre. Most importantly, the foregoing brief narrative provides in sociological terms some understanding of how the caucus events transpired. That is, it constitutes what Weber termed an interpretation of action in terms of its subjective meaning. However, a caveat is in order—although the contention of AFT caucuses shows a clear distinction of class, status group, and party orientations, the study of other organizations would probably exhibit more complex action. That is, numerous class, status group, and party-based orientations would likely be in contention. Nonetheless, use of ideal type, or sensitizing, concepts of these collectivities would provide a means of separating the various threads of meaningful action.

CHAPTER XIII

Conformation

Social structure, from the perspective of this essay, refers to the patterns of collective action exhibited by individuals in aggregates, groups, and organizations. As previously stated, organizations have structure—they have distinctive patterns of action, established ways of doing things. And, when one speaks of structure, one is choosing to focus on the constancy, the regularity of organizational action. As March and Simon opine, "Organization structure consists simply of those aspects of the pattern of behavior in the organization that are relatively stable and that change only slowly," (1958, p.170). Nonetheless, organizational structure is always somewhat in the process of change. Revisiting an earlier concept, organizational patterns are generally moving from one negotiated order to another. In organizational literature such change is usually seen as the product of problem solving, or adaptive behavior on the part of organizational participants. This is not to say the change is objectively rational, or rational from an overall perspective of the organization. And, situated individuals may not get the outcomes they seek, but typically they are attempting to deal with problems. Further, structure and structural change are not necessarily embodiments of organizational efficiency. Herein, it is problem

> Social structure ... refers to the patterns of collective action exhibited by individuals in aggregates, groups, and organizations.

solving and not organizational efficiency that is a more central criterion (axial principle) of organizational performance. Indeed, problem solving, or organizational intelligence in action, may occasionally require considerable inefficiency. However, Mead, pragmatists, and symbolic interactionists presumably, for the most part, concur that patterns of collective, rationally oriented action typically arise from problem solving. With respect to organizational theorists, Handel observes, "Classical administrative theory since Gulick argued that organizations emerge to solve problems of complex cooperation," (2003, p.264). In addition, the problem solving view of organizational structure is expressed by March and Simon, and by Chandler. March and Simon state, "It has been the central theme of this chapter that the basic features of organizational structure and function derive from the characteristics of human problem-solving processes and rational human choice," (1958, p.169). Chandler largely summarizes his classic study of the evolution of American corporate structure in remarking, "Expansion did cause administrative problems which led in time to organizational change and readjustment," (1993, p.380).

If problem solving may be seen as the major impetus to change in organizational structure, the question may be asked: who's problem, and who's solution? This, as previously discussed, is a matter of contention. Within this essay the concern is with collective action. Very simply, individual action without the support from some form of collectivity will likely have little impact on organizational processes. Lacking such support, individual intelligence about problems and their solutions will be lost to neglect or impotence. Collectivities—and included in this is the administrative group— sponsor utilitive, normative, and authoritive convictions about organizational practices. The question becomes: what collectivities are in contention over matters of organizational structure and structural change? Or, what collectivities are in contention over the definition of organizational problems and solutions? Different collectivities participating in an organization necessarily have somewhat different agendas for structural arrangements. A particular definition of a problem and its solution may be irrational for the organization as a whole, or for certain parts of the organization, but quite rational for a specific collectivity. Accordingly, collectivities, inside and out, engage in struggles to impose their brand of meaning on organizational action.

Recall that Weber said the structure of societies varies according to whether they are dominated by orders of class or status. He says, "Depending upon the prevailing mode of stratification, we shall speak of a 'status society' or a 'class society,'" (1978, p.306). And, had Weber lived longer and witnessed Nazi, Fascist, Stalinist, Maoist, and similar societies, he likely would have added party to this list. Similarly, a number of organizational theorists have suggested relationships between the dominant orientation to action and structural characteristics. For example, the principal orientation identified by Etzioni in his comparative study of organizations is type of compliance. With respect to structure Etzioni declares:

> *Organizations which differ in their compliance structure tend also to differ in the goals they pursue; in the kind, location, power, and interaction of their elites; in the level and kinds of consensus attained and in the communications and socialization employed to attain it; in recruitment, scope, and pervasiveness; and in the distribution and control of charismatic participants. Moreover, organizations which differ in their compliance structure tend also to differ in the way they allocate tasks and power over time. (1961, p.xv)*

Clarke and Wilson classify organizations according to the type of incentive for participation that is given the greatest emphasis. Scott remarks about Clarke and Wilson's work:

> *Like Etzioni (1961), whose similar typology was developed at the same time, Clarke and Wilson suggest that although all organizations use all three types of incentives, it is usually possible to identify a predominant type for each. And associated with each type are important structural and operational differences. (1998, p.173)*

When one speaks of differences among organizations with respect to structure, one is referring to patterns of activity associated with such things as the authority arrangement, the mode of stratification, the task structure or architecture of core activities, the means of socialization or training, the patterns of communication, and so forth. This essay follows Weber's lead and suggests that structure will likely vary according to whether class or class-like, status group or status group-like, or party or party-like orientations to action (i.e., attitudes) are dominant. Such collectivities will contend over the definition and prioritization of organizational problems and their solutions. Of course, structure will also vary according to particular expressions of class, status group, or party orientation—as the case may be. This conceptual approach appears to satisfy Perrow's criticism of organizational theories that feature typologies of organizations (1986, p.140). He says, "We desire typologies that will order the diversity of organizations in such a way that we can explain differences in structure and/ or goals. But if the typology is based on either structure or goals, we risk tautologies." The assertion, here, is that an organizational typology based on the dominance of class, status group, or party orientations and the variations of each can indeed give plausible explanations of structural differences. In addition, differences in structure may also exist among subunits of an organization. Frequently, different subunits have different prevailing orientations to action. For example, some departments or divisions, according to their particular orientations to action, may be decentralized while other are centralized. These subunits are essentially organized action within organized action. Of course, the validity of these assertions is an empirical question, which must be explored in actual circumstances.

Why does organizational structure tend to vary according to the type of meaning that is prevalent in action? It was said earlier that meaning pertains to the intended consequences, or perceived ends of action. On the other hand, structure, by and large, refers to the means by which ends are attained. In social action it is patterns of action directed to anticipated outcomes. Dewey agrees, "Structure is constancy of means, of things used for consequences," (1929, p.72). This essay asserts there is a stickiness of means and ends. The stickiness of means and ends is expressed, for example, in Mead's notion that one continuously reconstructs the past, and constructs the future, in the present's, meaningful action. That is, not just any past leads up to the present, as it is envisioned. Not just any action in the present will get to where one wants to be in the future. Mead further expressed the stickiness of means and ends in the concept that an object is a collapsed act. A chair is something one sits on. Alternatively, one may break it up, burn it in a fireplace or wood stove, and use it as something to keep warm. Yet again, one may sell the chair as a means to getting some cash. None of this is to say there is a determinate relationship between means and ends, between structure and orientation to action. Rather, a particular type of action may find certain structural elements to be more accommodating than the apparent alternatives. Conversely, particular structural arrangements may encourage an affinity for certain orientations to action. Referring back to an earlier discussion, the accommodation, or fit, of particular means and ends of social action is what Weber referred to as an elective affinity.

In a study of Weber's development and use of ideal type methodology, Heckman (1983) discusses his perspective on what is herein called the stickiness of orientations to action and patterns of action. Heckman says:

> *Weber always identifies an action by specifying its subjective meaning and by identifying the particular course of action that is linked to this meaning. Thus it is simply not the case that meaning determines action or vice versa; rather, meaning and action are linked, and both follow from identification of the action. (p.51)*

Heckman states that this perspective is characteristic of all of Weber's empirical works:

> *With regard to every structural analysis that he considers, Weber would argue that the structure would not be a particular type unless the dominant belief system were a corresponding type; and conversely, a particular kind of belief system is manifest in a particular structure. (p.57)*

Further, Heckman argues this perspective is critical to Weber's ideal type formation:

> *The relevance of the synthesis that Weber effects in the ideal type lies in the fact that, on the one hand, it is firmly rooted in the social actor's subjective meaning and, on the other hand, without losing this subjective grounding, it provides a tool for the structural analysis of social institutions. (p.15)*

So, means and ends of social action are tethered by meaning. Insofar as individuals function in a context of meaning, there is an affinity between means and ends of action. And, it seems that one cannot detach means and ends, altogether. This is not a matter of mechanical necessity, of a positivistic causal relationship, but, again, a matter of the meaning that individuals incorporate in social action. The stickiness of means and ends has to do with the consistency of meaning—which rests upon some coherence between the means and ends. There will be, at the least, some tension present if organizational means and ends are not consistent. Numerous proverbs and quotations express the common sense observation that means used in action must be compatible with the consequences of action. For example, Nelson Mandela said, "We cannot climb to freedom on the corpses of innocent people," (Keane, 2013). That is, one cannot climb to freedom by denying freedom. Yet, there is no necessity regarding structure and dominant meaning in an organization, only elective affinity.

Of course, there is struggle, as well. Individuals and groups will struggle over which—or who's—elective affinity will dominate. And, following the general theme of this essay, the struggle may be based on articulated interests, value preferences, or authority concerns, or any mix thereof.

If there is a change in the dominant meaning, the consequences regarded as most important in an organization, for whatever reason, one may anticipate related changes in the organization's architecture, its structure, what is herein termed its conformation. Examples of possible scenarios include the following: the privatization of a public or non-profit hospital, the ideological realignment of a political party, a Communist or mob takeover of a trade union, the adoption of a corporate business model by a charity, and a sectarian religious takeover of a local public school board. An example receiving widespread attention, at the present time, is the "corporatization" surge in American public higher education. This surge is also occurring in other professional and public service arenas. Declining state funding and other political developments have fostered a shift toward a corporate business model in public higher education. Much of American higher education appears to have been transforming over the last several decades from what one might call an academic or learning community model to a corporate business model. Traditionally higher education has featured many characteristics that are commonly associated with status groups and a status order. Higher education was defined by a long-standing academic culture and many academic subcultures. One could say there was an emphasis on traditions, communal relations, consensus decision making, knowledge as an end in itself, and identity as an elite within the greater society. Increasingly, higher education has taken on the trappings of American large-scale corporations. The changes bring to the fore market relationships, economic considerations, and class relations. At the same time, there is a diminution of community or status group relations. These changes are often discussed in blogs, newsletters, academic articles, and other media used by academia and an interested public. While the extent of change may be in dispute, the change is certainly a matter of contention at campuses across the United States, and also more broadly. And, there is little doubt as to the direction change has occurred. Presented herewith is an informal collection, a gleaming, of observations about the changes in

> There is no necessity regarding structure and dominant meaning in an organization, only elective affinity.

organizational structure associated with this shift of dominant orientation within American higher education.

Associated with the increasing adoption of a corporate business model (generically a class orientation) in American higher education, the following changes are alleged to have occurred:

» There has been a centralization of authority, of academic decision making. University administrators are unilaterally making decisions that respond to market concerns, rather than engaging in a process of collegial consultation and consensus-building. This includes making changes in curriculum and academic policies (Fichtenbaum, 2015b). It also extends to research agendas, the appointment of departmental chairs, and other traditional faculty matters (Westheimer, 2010).

» There has been a relative expansion of administrative staff and layers of administration. Mills stated, in 2012, that in the last thirty or forty years fulltime faculty has grown by fifty percent, similar to student enrollment, but the number of administrators has gone up by eighty-five percent, and administrative staff by about four times that. The highly regarded professor who takes a time-out to serve as an administrator, once common, is now an anachronism.

» Academic staff in universities have been increasingly differentiated into vertical layers. The percentage of full-time professors has steadily declined, and there is much greater reliance on adjuncts and instructors to teach undergraduate courses. Schmidlin (2015), citing AAUP figures, reports that non-tenure positions have gone up from twenty percent in 1970 to seventy-six percent by 2015.

» There has been a structural change in salaries, benefits, and job security. Increasingly university presidents are paid like major corporate CEOs, faculty salaries are diminishing relatively and showing greater inequality, the majority of faculty have no job security and few benefits, and many faculty are living below the federal poverty line (Fichtenbaum, 2015A;Schmidlin, 2015).

» There has been a shift from communal, or collegial, relations to contractual relations. Adjunct faculty are hired as part-time labor, and staff positions at bookstores, foodservices, and in janitorial and campus maintenance are increasingly outsourced to various contractors (Higgs, 2011). Of course, this allows an administration to reduce salary costs and shed responsibility for employee benefits. Also, course syllabi are taking on the characteristics of contractual relations between professors and students (Schuman, 2004).

» The corporatization of higher education has brought the imposition of corporate-style financial controls. In particular this means a push for numbers, for metrics that fit with market calculations. This is said to discourage or marginalize the consideration of broader academic, liberal arts values (Catropa, 2014; Cox, 2013).

» Universities provide greater rewards to departments and faculty that are entrepreneurial, that generate income. It is said that "publish or perish" has been supplanted by "publish, patent, or perish," (Cox, 2013). And, merit-based rewards have pushed colleagues apart, diminishing the sense of community (Westheimer, 2010).

» Following the business corporation model, many universities have become multinational organizations, setting up extensive operations overseas. This includes instructional, research, and corporate alliances, and arrangements with foreign governments to extend market reach (Lane, 2015).

» Many universities have greatly expanded their marketing activities. They compete for market share, attempt to establish highly-regarded brands, and hire marketing consultants to aid in these pursuits (Delblanco, 2007).

» There is a noticeable shift in the curriculum from liberal education to providing students with marketable skills. The shift to an emphasis upon vocational and professional training undermines the provision of a broad liberal arts education (Fichtenbaum, 2015b).

» Students are increasingly regarded as "customers." Universities divert resources to such things as entertainment centers, luxury dorms, food courts, and other accoutrements to enhance customer experience (Mills, 2012). State universities neglect the needs of within-state students, marketing to out-of-state and foreign students who pay much higher tuitions and fees (Mortensen, 2012).

» One may argue that the corporatization of public universities has the effect of stifling the free flow of ideas. The shift to a profit motive and an increased emphasis on securing patents places a premium upon security and withholding information. With stronger ties to corporate business, research tends to be narrow, short-term, and specific in its aims—perhaps hindering more significant advances. Certainly this development is contrary to past norms of academia and science (Chomsky, 2011).

Thus, it appears that a change in the meaning ascribed to actions on university campuses is accompanied by significant changes in the patterns of action. All of the summarized reports, from the front, so to speak, suggest strongly that a change in the dominant meaning from academic community values to market values leads to significant changes in the structure of campus action. Said otherwise, there is a shift from the dominance of status group affinities to class considerations. It is not addressed here, but obviously one would also expect the obverse, a change in structure, in patterns of activity, would encourage a shift in the meaning ascribed to action by individuals. One can imagine a variety of circumstances that would illustrate such a process. Also not addressed is the fact that the change on university campuses—as discussed above—involves a prolonged struggle among various class, status group, and party collectivities. With respect to conflict over corporatization, the author of this essay has personally observed, on one campus, power struggles between the administration and a faculty union, economic contention between departments that prosper and those that are left behind, disputes among groups with different professional views on the aims of higher education, and many other examples of contention. The topic is obviously worthy of extended study. However, the overriding point, here, is the stickiness of patterns of action and the meaning attributed to action. And, it is a mutual, two-way stickiness. This stickiness, once again, is what Weber referred to as an elective affinity. And, as previously mentioned, Mead agreed there is a necessary consonance between ideas and the structure of action. This discussion of corporatization in higher education has necessarily been a brief overview based largely secondary sources of information. If one were to pursue a detailed ethnography of a particular case, very likely a complex struggle involving class interests, status group value systems, and various party alignments would emerge. That analysis would provide a more adequate interpretative understanding of contention over the corporatization process.

CHAPTER XIV

Commitment

Organized action, as with all collective action, must be understood as the action of individuals. This idea was discussed earlier in terms of methodological individualism. Aggregates, groups, organizations do not, in and of themselves, engage in action. Yet, the interaction of individuals in such collectivities often does produce, in time, transformative, emergent qualities. How is it, then, that individuals come to participate in organized action? This is a matter of particular concern to those who create and maintain organizations. It relates to such activities as employee recruitment and retention; union organizing; attracting volunteers for hospitals or museums; membership development for professional, civic or fraternal organizations; proselytizing for religious congregations; and sustaining college and university alumni associations. Of particular relevance to this concern, and to the perspective presented in this essay, is the work cited earlier by Peter B. Clarke and James Q. Wilson (1961). They set forth a conceptual model that largely fits with the ideas of Weber and Mead, and they recognize the similarity of their incentive model to Weber's concepts of stratification. However, they specifically address political organizations and the incentives that attract and hold their participants. Accordingly, some of the distinctions they make may benefit from a rephrasing when applied to organizations in general.

In a book that expands upon their article, Wilson identifies four general kinds of incentives—or three kinds and one of these has two variations (1995, p.30–51).

Material incentives are tangible rewards such as money, or things and services readily treated as money. Specific solidary incentives are intangible, non-material rewards available to selected individuals in an organization. Examples would be individual status or power. Collective solidary incentives are intangible rewards that are collectively enjoyed by all members of an organization. Examples are fun, conviviality, and group status. Both forms of solidary incentives come from associating with one another in organizations and are non-material. The final incentive is purpose, which relates to the organization's objectives. Purposive incentives refer to the satisfaction of having contributed to a worthwhile political cause. In the present essay the two types of solidary incentives are merged into one, as both are characteristic of status group solidarity. This essay also rephrases the purposive incentive to refer more broadly to one's regard for the governing authority and its program for the organization. The result is an approximation of the economic, social-cultural, and political-authority dimensions of meaning used throughout this essay.

The Wilson and Clarke schema of incentives has become "quasi-canonical," or widely accepted, in many subsequent studies (Mansbridge, 1990, p.13). However, as mentioned earlier, Wilson and Clarke invoke exchange theory to explain the tie between an organization and an individual. Wilson contends, "The use of incentives to secure contributions of time, money, or effort involves an exchange relationship between an association and its supporters," (1995, p.238). Unfortunately an exchange model is not fully compatible with the perspective in this essay. The Wilson and Clarke incentives must be recast in terms more consistent with the previously identified dimensions of meaning. Accordingly, one may state that individuals voluntarily participate in organized action due to the consequences they anticipate from doing so. That is, they participate in organizations because of the meaning they ascribe to such participation. Now, this may be a matter of exchange which serves their material interests. Thus, it may be an utilitive orientation, action directed to material ends. However, participation in an organization may be a matter of expressing and sharing culture, i.e., beliefs, values, norms, and the solidarity thereby experienced. That is, it largely serves ideal ends. Thirdly, the orientation to action may be a matter of allegiance to an authority that is viewed as legitimate. This could be posited as an affinity to the means of organized action (i.e., an authority system), with perhaps little regard for material or ideal ends. As suggested before, an extraordinarily strong attraction to the means of organization may be viewed as charismatic in nature. In contrast, the first two orientations are probably most often found in rational and traditional authority contexts, respectively. This is a matter of elective affinity. It should be added that empirically these ideal type incentives are always of a mixed nature.

Additional authors have brought forward tri-part models of how individuals are attracted to organized action. Weber, as cited in Bendix, recognized how interests, ideas, and political authority orientations give rise to collective action. Again, this is evident in his tri-part theory of stratification and his tri- part theory of authority. Also mentioned earlier, Mead saw how three early types of generalized attitudes of other produce collective action. Quoted earlier, the organization theorists Katz and Kahn relate, in their own terms, how task-related, authority, and social considerations may contribute to organized action. Etzioni distinguished three types of organizations according to the kind of power that is predominantly used to induce participants to carry out organizational action. According to the means employed to ensure compliance, he identifies coercive, remunerative, and normative forms of power. His typology largely agrees with that used in this essay, except that he limits authority to compulsion. Finally, just to show the breadth of possible comparisons, there is McClelland's typology of needs characteristic of individuals: achievement, affiliation, and power (1961, passim). It takes little imagination to see how the needs identified by McClelland correspond to the three dimensions of meaning suggested in this essay. The point, here, is that in one guise or another, comparable distinctions with respect to the meaning individuals find in organized action appear throughout organizational and related literature.

One of the difficulties noted with the Wilson and Clarke incentive model is that its terms, its concepts, are difficult to operationalize. Setting aside a dispute over the use of variables, appropriately raised by Blumer (1954), the point is that Wilson and Clarke's concepts are difficult to use in empirical research. From a positivist perspective it is hard to turn them into quantitative measures and do so with some sense of reliability and validity. That will not be attempted here; however one can use fairly equivalent terms in a symbolic interactionist perspective, avoid positivist difficulties, and produce an interpretative understanding of collective action. One way to do this is by defining incentives in terms of the identifying characteristics, or what one may call the "indicators," of class, status group, and party. Recall that class, status group, and party were earlier discussed as sources of collective action. Accordingly, the identifying traits of class, status group, and party may also serve as sensitizing concepts for identifying incentives, or types of meaning, that attract and hold organizational participants. For example, within the organizational structure one may distinguish class or class-like aggregates of organizational participants, in which the individuals have a set of common objective interests. Recalling Weber, we know that such interests are identifying characteristics of class, associated with particular positions in a task structure and related exchange relations. However, these interests are also very likely economic, or utilitive, incentives for individuals to participate in organized action. Individuals are drawn to organizational action that serves their interests. Again, within the cultural realm one may distinguish sub-cultural groupings—status or status-like groups—each of which has distinctive ideas, i.e., beliefs, values, norms. Such ideas and related practices, as well as the recognized standing of such groups, are identifying characteristics of status or status-like groups. However, these ideas and related practices—their expression and sharing—are also very likely normative incentives for organizational participation. That is, most individuals are drawn to activities that agree with their beliefs, express their values, or comply with their norms. Finally, relating to the authority system of an organization, one may distinguish party or party-like groups endeavoring to influence or perhaps hold authority. The identifying characteristics of parties are the things they struggle over with respect to collective decision making. Cited earlier, these are such things as selecting leaders, defining objectives, forming policy, outlining strategy and tactics, and so forth, and they may be authoritive incentives for organizational participation. That is, organizational participants are drawn to activities in which the leadership views and organizational objectives and policies match their own. Thus, the defining characteristics of class, status group, and party can also serve as sensitizing concepts, helping one identify and test incentives for participation. They offer a means to explore individual commitment to organizational action.

A major caveat is in order—before considering in further detail possible incentives for attracting and retaining members of an organization. There is no substitute for effective communication from organizational leaders. Capable leaders will learn how to take the "attitude of the other," how to reach into the minds of organizational participants and effectively communicate the meaning of participation. They will be able to speak to participants in their own voice, using the relevant incentives to share their interests, share their cultural views, and share their sense of purpose. Doing so is an exercise of reflexive intelligence. As with all reflexive action it requires standing outside of oneself, carefully objectifying one's action from the viewpoints of selected others, and trying alternative actions. In some circles it's called salesmanship. In others it is called leadership. Nonetheless, presented below are three synopses of potential incentives for organizational participation. Although they may appear to be narrowly defined, this is not without purpose. They are for possible use in analysis; they are not empirical claims. They are based on the assumption that Weber's concepts may be useful at any level of analysis.

The items discussed below suggest with considerable variety—as sensitizing concepts—the kinds of class, status group, or party characteristics one may find useful as utilitive, normative, or authoritive incentives for organizational participation. They indicate a breadth of opportunity to innovate, to try alternative incentives, and to assess their effectiveness. Many additional items could be mentioned, and the relevance of any particular item will depend entirely on the context of organizational action. The main point, here, is that each item, in an appropriate context, serves as one indicator of class, status group, or party, and also is a possible incentive for participation. Poorly handled by an organization, each item may be a disincentive. Presented first are possible indicators of class, the types of interests that may be shared by organizational participants who occupy a common material situation, i.e., an aggregate of individuals in similar task and exchange relationships. Each of these meets Weber's criteria of class, albeit on a lower level of analysis than he typically employed. That is, they are material interests and related to an exchange process. The point is that an aggregate of individuals who share, for example, the same wage category, e.g., the minimum wage, may for analytic purposes be considered a class. This depends upon the situation. It is not to say that they occupy a broadly recognized social class. If one prefers, one may use a term such as a "micro-class."

A favorable or unfavorable circumstance with respect any one of the following indicators—if it applies—may affect an individual's organizational commitment. As to being indicators of class standing, these are items that frequently appear in collective bargaining, when a union represents a particular collection of workers with common tasks and exchange relations. Any of the enumerated task or exchange characteristics may become the basis of collective action by members of a union. Perhaps the most common material incentive is income such as wages, salary, bonuses, and occasionally profit sharing. Added to income are benefits such as health, life, dental, vision, or disability insurance, retiree benefits, IRAs, and stock options. Of no small consideration is paid released time such as holiday, sick time, vacation, child care, family, medical, bereavement, and sabbatical leave. Looking to the future, participants may be interested in items such as opportunities for promotion, learning new skills, education release time, tuition reimbursement, and simply employment security. What may be termed perquisites, or fringe benefits, may include items such as an expense account, transportation assistance in the form of parking, rail or bus pass, use of a company automobile, subsidized air travel, credit union membership, health or exercise club membership, a charitable giving match, leisure or vacation programs, professional services such as legal, tax preparation, on-site medical, adoption assistance, or mortgage placement. Various conditions or resources may considered a plus, such as organizational facilities, working conditions, the provision of housing, meals, clothing, computer or cell phone, a convenient work location, flexible hours of work, being able to work from home, on-site child care, or a pet-friendly environment. What makes such items class indicators, or perhaps micro-class indicators, is whether or not they identify material interests and exchange relationships that pertain to an aggregate of individuals and—one may add— may become a basis for collective action. Certainly in the case of trade unions one can see that such items may designate a category of employees with various material concerns and these may lead to union actions. It should be added that many of the items could also pertain to organizational volunteers. In either case, the concern here is recognizing in items such as these possible clues or sensitizing indicators of class-oriented action.

Now, a discussion of the kinds of things a culture, or subculture, comprises within an organization. These are typical characteristics of a status group, say an ethnic group, or a group with a regionally-defined culture. How an organization acts with respect to any of the following, or other such items, may accord or not accord with the cultural attitudes and practices of those in a particular status or status-like group. Such action may thereby act as normative incentives or disincentive for participation. In the first instance, status groups are characterized by the ideas—the beliefs, values, and norms— that they convey. In addition they typically have a sense of identity, a sense of community, a sense of group prestige or standing, and may have an explicit code of honor. Status groups possess special ceremonies, rituals, holidays, group symbols, perhaps a special language, very likely a geographic "center," a group story or narrative, distinctive clothing, food, music, dance, and perhaps a literature or theatre. Status groups may have group heroes, group villains, occult or mystical practices, esoteric knowledge, special artifacts, and a practice of excluding non members. In addition, status groups typically assert a claim of superiority in some respect, and tend to denigrate other status groups. In an organizational setting a positive recognition and perhaps a sharing or enabling of status group characteristics may serve as a source of bonding, an inducement, an incentive for participation. Disparagement will likely produce a negative reaction. For the purpose of analysis—which is the prime consideration in this essay—such items may serve as sensitizing concepts, as signifiers of status group action and aid in the interpretative understanding of organizational action.

And finally, here are some possible authoritive incentives. They are the objectives, the sought-after outcomes, the meanings of participation often shared by party members, particularly party cadre. One may see them as characteristics that signify the existence of a party, and differences with respect such items will distinguish one party from another. Thus, a struggle over items such as those that follow may be indicative of party action. Should some the items appear to be no more than common management functions, recall that earlier in this essay an organization's administration was designated a party—the party in control. Among the things identifying parties and drawing individuals into party action are struggles over defining an organizational mission, designating organizational goals or objectives, electing leaders, appointing officials or staff, setting priorities for the use of organizational resources, setting an agenda—which often controls many important actions— adopting organizational strategy and tactics, establishing organizational rules and policies, adjudicating and enforcing rules, adopting revenue provisions, establishing external relations or alliances, mediating internal conflicts, passing legislation, and so on. As with all party action, such items may reflect class interests or status group ideas, as well as party aspirations. Handled well, such items may become incentives, may draw individuals into participation. Handled poorly they may become disincentives. As discussed earlier, within the context of the AFT conventions and delegate relations, they were matters of great interest—and sometimes intense dispute—by delegates. They were the kinds of things over which the AFT parties had spirited contention. And, as interviews for the AFT caucus study indicated, they were of great and lasting meaning to many participants.

Again, what is being said here is that the indicators, or characteristics, of class, of status group, and of party may serve as leads, as sensitizing concepts, for identifying likely incentives to attract and retain organizational participants. The indicators thus do double duty—they help identify class, status group, or party action, and they identify possible incentives for attracting organizational participants. Or, if one prefers, they provide a means of operationalizing incentives for organizational participation. Now, it stands to reason that if participants, or potential participants, may realize their interests, their values, their allegiances through organizational participation they will be attracted to such participation. Organizational leaders, exercising reflexive intelligence in attracting and retaining participants, may use various indicators of class, status group, and party to identify and systematically test (i.e., experimentally) existing or possible incentives for participation. In so doing, they may reach beyond narrow conceptions of the meaning, or consequences of action, that draw individuals into collective action. Attractions to organizational participation are multidimensional, and one may assume that effective organizations explore and utilize each of the several dimensions of meaning.

As an illustration of reconstructing incentives for members, consider the American Federation of Teachers in the aftermath of the 1960s breakthrough in collective bargaining. This was a period of extraordinary growth in members and local affiliates. Initially the union's main focus was on issues of class and authority. A substantial part of the union's activity was directed at achieving material gains for teachers—salary increases, improved benefits, and such. AFT organizers unabashedly claimed that the union could do much better than rival organizations in improving teachers' standard of living. In addition, the AFT aggressively pursued authority—legitimate power—as the legal representative of teachers in collective bargaining and related matters. This involved winning collective bargaining elections, bargaining contracts, administering the contracts, and other aspects of the struggle for power (i.e., party action) to establish the union's authority. However, as this process matured, AFT leaders increasingly recognized a need to develop the union's professional (i.e., status group) activities. Referring to AFT President Albert Shanker, Kahlenberg (p. 304) recounts:

> *In organizing campaigns, Shanker's blunt talk about the need to reform education and improve teacher quality had its risks. AFT organizer Phil Kugler says some saw Shanker as "bashing" teachers. At the same time, by the mid-1980s, polls were showing that younger members in particular were less concerned about bread-and-butter issues and more concerned about teacher professionalism. During recruitment drives, AFT organizers would wave the American Educator—with its thoughtful articles on cultural literacy and phonics— and emphasize the AFT's strong professional development department to point out differences with the NEA.*

Organizational leaders face a continuing challenge to evaluate and perhaps restructure the incentives that attract and retain participants. In the case of the AFT, discussed above, the union vastly expanded its staff and programs centering upon professional issues of concern to teachers. This had the benefit not only of making the union more attractive to teachers, but it also greatly improved the AFT's public image.

A multidimensional approach offers the prospect of strengthened bonds between members and an organization. Conversely, ignoring the dimensions of meaning foregoes additional strength and opens the door to various forms of disunity. In using a dimensional approach the recruitment and retention program of an organization will be, in sociological terms, stratified throughout. It will likely be more comprehensive, recognizing a broad spectrum of incentives, or forms of meaning. It will likely be more systematic, providing a methodical way of considering alternative incentives. Most important, it will likely be more analytic, supporting a reflexive process of problem solving, a rational establishment of organizational means to organizational ends. At the very least, an overview of indicators may provide checklists against which organizational leaders may assess their response to participants' concerns.

CHAPTER XV.

Comprehension

Having arrived at this last section, what ground has been covered, where has one arrived? This essay outlined a synthesis of Max Weber and George Herbert Mead's principal ideas. It has put forward a symbolic interactionist perspective for the analysis of complex organizations, or large-scale social action. It has, in the process, suggested a comprehensive view of organizational theory. With regard to the synthesis, there is correspondence of Mead and Weber's concepts at many points. Here are some examples:

> » There is a comparability of Weber's elective affinity and Mead's view that coherence of meaning is the glue, so to speak, of social structures. Enduring social relations are held together by an accepted and continuously reaffirmed, meaningful association of the means and ends of social action.

> » There is a comparability of Weber's three orders –class, status, and legal—with Mead's early universals. Each recognizes the economic, social/cultural, and political/authority dimensions of meaning as fundamental in social action.

> » There is a comparable emphasis upon reflexivity and rationality in social action. At different levels of analysis the focus is upon the purposeful structuring of means and ends of social behavior.

> » There is a comparability of Mead's me, other, and I with Weber's class, status group, and party concepts. They refer to the ongoing structure

of action, the subjective consideration of action, and the construction of purposeful action.

» There is a comparability of Weber's concept of charisma and the emergent properties of Mead's I. Each is seen as unpredictable, innovative, and essentially reconstructive of ongoing action.

» There is a comparability of Weber's ideal types and Blumer's sensitizing concepts, derived from Mead. Each is designated not as concrete entities but as guides to inquiry—qualitative inquiry.

In addition to these, and other, similarities of concepts, there are important similarities in Mead and Weber's perspectives on social science. Some examples follow:

» There is a clear rejection of any concept of causal laws in social action.

» Human social action is teleological. That is, meaningful action is action directed to participants' expected outcomes.

» There is a rejection of the idea that only behavior which is directly observable, or purely objective, can be dealt with scientifically. Social phenomena necessarily have both subjective and objective properties—and neither is primary.

» Inquiry is directed to achieving an interpretative understanding of social action. Social action is undecipherable without thoroughly delving into the meaning it has for participants.

» Priority is given to qualitative methodology, in order to get at the meaning of action. Quantitative methods are viewed not as superior, but as supportive of qualitative inquiry.

» Qualitative distinctions are produced within human interaction, and are not imposed from an external source.

» Meaningful interaction creates emergent properties, largely arising from problem solving behavior. Social entities have properties not accounted for by a sum of the parts.

» The social world is viewed as constructed and continuously reconstructed by participants. It does not have an independent, objective existence. It is subject to a continuous, multi-dimensional struggle over the prevailing meaning of action.

» All social action is the action of individuals—groups, organizations, institutions, and societies do not act. Nevertheless, they have real effect if defined as real, and one can productively generalize about collectivities of individuals and construct concepts for that purpose.

> » Both reductionism and structuralism are rejected. Other than some form of acceptance by participants, there are no limits to the possible variety of social arrangements.

> » Any concept of truth or validity refers only to ideas which appear to hold up when tested in action. That is, it is a pragmatic conception of truth.

> » The ultimate goal of social scientific inquiry is to increase the capacity for reflexivity, or rationality, in social action. There is no expectation of prediction and control, as in natural science.

> » Scientific inquiry is simply a highly rationalized form of normal human intelligence.

> » In sum, there is a complete rejection of positivism in social science. The social world is not a mechanical construction to be studied in the manner of natural sciences.

What ideas, what advice is available for using the proposed synthesis of Mead and Weber for conducting social research? Here the focus is on using the ideal types of class, status group, and party—or their surrogates—in an organizational context. With that in mind, it is the author's experience that the perspective of the proposed synthesis is useful in many ways, for example:

> » With respect to organizations it may be used for a comparative study of organizations in terms of dominant meaning and structure; to study organizational change; to study the formation and development of organizations; to do assessments of "organizational alignment," to study organizational power struggles; to study the internal groupings that mediate or transmit external influences on an organization, etc.

> » With respect to politics and legislation it may be used to study the struggle over legislation; to study the formation or dissolution of coalitions; to study electoral support in campaigns; to study the use of wedge issues; etc.

> » With respect to commitment by organizational participants it may be used to study the recruitment and retention of members or volunteers, it may be used for client or customer loyalty programs; and particularly it may be used for market segmentation in marketing campaigns; etc.

Again, the above examples pertain to the effects of class, status group, and party affinities within organizations. However, it is the author's conviction that the symbolic interactionist perspective discussed in this essay can be broadly applied in research. But, how does one proceed in a typical study? Typically one begins with a desire to explain what is considered a significant social event. The aim is to understand it; perhaps to compare it to one or more other events. Any significant event is generally the action of a number, perhaps a great number, of individuals. One assumes there are some underlying patterns of collective action. It is important to set about learning all one can about the event. This means constructing a descriptive, factual account—most likely a comprehensive narrative of the event. The account, or narrative, must be based on information from participants, using standard interpretative methods. These include participant observation, ethnography, interviews, documents, and so forth. As one builds the narrative, one continuously looks for patterns in the action. In particular, one looks for patterns that appear to involve aggregate, group, or organized action. Participants are asked about patterns and their meaning. Key to identifying and understanding these patterns are sensitizing concepts, or ideal types (e.g., class, status group, and party, or their approximations), that suggest where to look and what to look for. One may also explore these patterns in terms of the social-psychology of participants. That is, one seeks to ground the meaning of action in examples of reflexive, individual experience.

As the building of a narrative continues, one continuously adds, rejects, modifies, constructs, etc., ideal type or sensitizing concepts that appear useful in explaining the event. And, as the ideal type or sensitizing concepts are brought in to summarize and explain action—to discern patterns of meaningful action— it is important to seek out factual information that will critically test the fit of the ideal types. For example, in the previously discussed case of the AFT caucuses, the fact that the Progressive Caucus locals were deliberately exclusionary was—again citing Weber—a critical test of the status group orientation. One could say this information was a clinching fact. Now, the objective of the narrative is to summarize the patterns of action and their meaning. The aim is to account for, to meaningfully interpret, all of the threads of action that an event comprises. In so doing, one can aim for what Weber called a

> What Weber called a casually adequate explanation ... in Mead's terms ... would be a fully reflexive understanding of the event.

causally adequate explanation. That is, an explanation that embraces both the objective facts and the subjective meaning. In Mead's terms it would be a fully reflexive understanding of the event.

In conclusion, this essay has outlined a theoretical perspective integrating the ideas of Max Weber and George Herbert Mead, demonstrated a symbolic interactionist method to analyze large social processes, and presented a holistic approach to the study of complex organizations. Based as it is on the ideas of Mead and Weber, it may yet appear a radical interpretation of their ideas. In rejoinder one may say that too often scholarship on Mead and Weber, particularly scholarship with positivist inclinations, has not fully appreciated the radical potential of their ideas. Within this essay the author has attempted to stay within the bounds of Mead's and Weber's own expositions of their ideas. Whatever the essay's limitations, and surely there are many, it nonetheless proposes that a synthesis of Mead's and Weber's ideas is the most promising way forward for sociology.

AFT Caucus History,

1934–1970

CONDENSED FROM "TEACHERS AND UNION
DEMOCRACY," PH.D. THESIS, HARVARD
UNIVERSITY, 1977, BY GERALD D. MORRIS

From the time of its formation in 1916, the American Federation of Teachers (AFT) was divided by political cleavages. Generally there were two major factions, identified by participants as the conservative and liberal wings of the union. The conservative faction was usually led by a Chicago union local; whereas the liberal faction was usually led by the New York City local. Typically the two factions disagreed on social issues of the day, or on the AFT's relationship with the American Federation of Labor (AFL). However, the two factions were just loose collections of like-minded convention delegates. The Chicago leaders and their followers from other cities admired the AFL's leaders as "fine and practical men." Conversely, the New York City local's leaders repeatedly opposed the AFL leaders on social policy and sometimes supported challengers to the incumbent AFL leaders. The AFT's national office was located in Chicago, but the union's official journal was edited and published in New York City. This led to constant strife over both the activities of the national office and the policies espoused in the journal. The journal was considered too radical by the leaders in Chicago, as it reflected socialist and pacifist views popular in the New York City local. With regard to the national office, from the mid-1920s until the mid-1950s, much of the struggle was over the selection and supervision of the AFT secretary- treasurer, the union's only full-time official. When the liberal faction was nominally in control of the union—a majority on the executive council—the Chicago-based secretary-treasurer would "put the brakes" on their activist agenda. Typifying the struggle, in the mid-1930s a New York City convention delegate charged that the conservative leadership in the national office had been too practical and not sufficiently idealistic. Speaking for the other side, a delegate from Chicago countered that the New York City local contained an active group of Communists.

In the early 1930s a secretary-treasurer was installed by the liberal faction. However, this was a short-lived victory. The secretary-treasurer used her position in the national office to establish her independence and to control the union. In successive conventions the liberal faction began introducing measures to reorganize the national office and curtail the powers of the secretary-treasurer. The secretary-treasurer outmaneuvered the New York led faction, particularly by exploiting loose provisions in the AFT constitution. The AFT constitution made it very easy to charter new locals. Furthermore, to encourage new locals it gave them vastly disproportionate representation in AFT conventions. Additionally, such locals could easily send proxies for convention votes. Thus, the situation was ripe for the secretary-treasurer to encourage and formally recognize a considerable number of "paper locals," collect their proxies for convention voting, and significantly shift the union's balance of power. When the liberal faction came to the 1934 convention, thinking they were prepared to remove the secretary-treasurer, it was they who were removed. They lost control of the union's presidency and executive council. The secretary-treasurer, in combination with a peculiar combination of conservative and ultra-left delegates, controlled the convention. Following their defeat, the liberal faction held a meeting and formed a semi-secret body, the Confidential Conference. The aim of the Confidential Conference was to promote reforms within the AFT: elimination of proxy voting, the reduction of disproportionate representation of small locals, closer control over chartering new locals, and election of the secretary-treasurer. The Confidential Conference was simply oriented to promoting certain reforms, not to gaining power in the union.

The reform proposals of the Confidential Conference were rebuffed at the succeeding 1935 convention. Again, the convention was controlled by a coalition of conservative and ultra-left delegates, based in part on paper locals. AT the 1935 convention, the issue of Communist influence in the New York City local became an open fight. In desperation, the New York City old guard sought to have their own charter revoked, so a new local could be formed. Again, the liberal faction lost. The opposing faction was exceedingly well organized. In particular, the Communists and other left-wing groups were seasoned in the arts of convention manipulation. In contrast, the liberal group was naïve. Also, the AFT activists were accustomed to labels, such as Communist, being pinned on teacher unionists by labor's opponents and were accordingly skeptical. Near the end of the 1935 AFT convention the members of the Confidential Conference withdrew in protest. They held a meeting to plan further action and formed the first organized caucus, or party, within the AFT. Renamed the Ringdahl Caucus, after their new leader from New Bedford, Massachusetts, they realized they were engaged in a struggle to control the union. In contrast to the opposing faction, which included a political spectrum from conservative to Communist, the Ringdahl Caucus was not based simply on the expediency of trading votes. Its members shared the liberal-left philosophy which had long been expressed in the union by the New York led faction. Eventually, the Ringdahl Caucus would become an open caucus, endorse and campaign for candidates, develop a platform to state its views, solicit support, and assemble a political apparatus strong enough to gain control of the union.

After the 1935 convention, Communists gained control of the New York City local, ultimately the Philadelphia local and several others, and organized locals not composed primarily of public school teachers. This greatly increased their numbers, and the 1936 convention probably represented the peak of Communist influence in the AFT. A number of resolutions were passed supporting Communist policies and endorsing Communist "front" organizations. Communist Party literature was freely circulated at the convention and most of the convention speakers made remarks that paralleled the Communist Party line. Among AFT insiders, the 1936 convention was often referred to as the "Red Convention." Following the 1936 convention, the Ringdahl Caucus reorganized as the Public School Caucus. This emphasized their membership base in public schools, in contrast to the opposing caucus's lesser support from public school personnel. At the 1937 convention, some of the conservative locals moved over to the liberal's Public School Caucus. Ordinarily disinterested in ideological disputes, the conservatives were increasingly alarmed by the union's Communist-influenced journal, which was mailed directly to their members. Control began to gradually shift away from the Communist-led faction, as conservative locals defected in succeeding conventions. The showdown came with the 1939 convention, known as The First Battle of Buffalo, as it was held in Buffalo, New York. An important world event took place during the convention and created disunity in the Communist-led faction. For years the Communists had called for a "united front" against fascism. Suddenly, overnight, the Communist line changed, as Hitler and Stalin signed a non-aggression pact. Overnight, the Communists in the AFT followed the Communist Party line, supporting the alliance with Hitler. This abrupt, unprincipled shift in a long-established, core policy cost the Communists much of their support within the AFT.

At the 1939 AFT convention, the liberal caucus began to "grow up." Changing its name to the Progressive Caucus, the caucus adopted new tactical procedures. Floor leaders were chosen, as were speakers for various issues, and other organizing measures were initiated. Control shifted slightly to the Progressive Caucus. It did not achieve a majority on the executive council, but it did elect as president, George Counts, a Columbia University professor, noted critic of the Communist Party, and one of the most influential educators in the United States. He, along with John Dewey and John Childs, also from Columbia University—all active in support of the AFT and teacher unionism—had a large influence on the AFT's liberal faction. At the 1940 convention, known as The Second Battle of Buffalo, the Progressive Caucus made great strides and assumed complete control of the union. This was aided by another jolt in the Communist-led faction. During the 1940 Convention delegates heard of the assassination of Leon Trotsky in Mexico. The news shattered much of the Communist-led faction's support, as the Communists no longer appeared to be victims, but the perpetrators of aggression. Also of great importance in the 1940 convention was the unsparing organization of the Progressive Caucus. At the convention the caucus established: a "grape vine" to rapidly disseminate information, a service group to prepare materials for the convention floor, a resolutions committee to prepare issue positions, caucus floor leaders, designated speakers, and so forth. Most importantly—and this according to a number of participants—for the first time they had a new decision procedure. One participant said when interviewed, "When the meeting opened it was explained to you that you couldn't leave. If you were going to leave, you left now, see, before we got down to business. And, if you wanted to go visit other caucuses that was your business, but if you stayed in the meeting you were bound by the decisions the caucus made, unless you stood up publicly in the meeting and said you couldn't go along, because we were counting noses and votes. And fortunately we were so strict about it, that's one reason we licked them."

After the 1940 convention, strife continued over the Communist dominated locals. New York was expelled and several others fell by the wayside. However, the issue continued to dog AFT conventions, as Communist sympathizers sought to reinstate locals or raised various Communist-inclined issues. A new local was chartered in New York City, and it soon became the leader of the liberal faction. World War Two suspended regular AFT conventions for several years. In 1948, the anti-Communist unity wore off and the Progressive Caucus split into the liberal-left Progressive Caucus and the moderate- conservative National Caucus, or sometimes called the Classroom Teachers Caucus. Ostensibly, the split was over the selection of a union president. In any case, the alignment went back to the liberal vs. conservative cleavage, long present in the union. During the 1950s the alignment was pretty much Chicago, Atlanta, Cleveland, Toledo, and other mid-West locals in the National/ Classroom Teachers' Caucus. The liberal alignment was pretty much New York City, Philadelphia, Boston, Washington, D.C., Minneapolis-St. Paul, St. Louis, Detroit, Portland, Oregon. Immediately after the war there was an effort, particularly by the liberal group, to discontinue the highly organized caucuses. But, a variety of events demonstrated that was not feasible; there was no going back. So, by 1948, certainly by the early 1950s, caucuses were accepted as an inevitable part of AFT conventions. According to one interviewee, new delegates were told, "It's a good system, we said, and there are two great caucuses, just as in the national picture there are two great parties."

During the 1950s, control shifted back and forth, and new locals and leaders emerged in the two caucuses. Perennial issues were the AFT's organizing program and the editorial policy of the journal, American Teacher. The Progressive Caucus locals favored an aggressive, nationally-driven organizing program. The National Caucus locals viewed such a program as unwise and doomed to failure. It was said that the Progressive Caucus wanted a "far-flung seeding operation, whereas the National Caucus thought the only thing that worked was a grassroots program in which a strong local helps near-by teacher groups. The latter was referred to as "the mother hen and her chicks." The main disagreement in the 1950s was how to deal with the handful of racially segregated locals in the AFT. In a few cities the AFT had segregated locals, dating from the early days of the union. Neither caucus supported segregation, in any form, but they differed significantly on how best to handle the problem. The National Caucus, which included several large segregated locals, favored a gradual approach.

They believed forced integration would simply destroy the locals—as shortly it did. The teacher union locals could not be expected to get too far out in from of their communities. Here it must be added that the ever-pragmatic National Caucus locals depended upon close working relationships with local political officials. They disdained union militancy, in favor of accommodation with city or county officials. The liberal locals in the Progressive Caucus argued that segregation was undemocratic, contrary to the AFT constitution, and a scar on public education. Moreover, as idealists and activists, they would not let up on the issue. In this context it should be recalled that in the 1930s the AFT twice moved its convention—walking out of hotels—when some delegates experienced racial discrimination. Also, the AFT had joined legal cases, including filing an amicus brief with the Supreme Court in the Brown vs. Board of Education Case.

The members of the Progressive Caucus tended to view the AFT as part of a broad social movement based on organized labor which sought to bring about progressive changes in society. Members of the National / Classroom Teachers' Caucus viewed the AFT primarily as a pragmatic means of promoting public education, particularly at the local level, and improving the working conditions and salaries of teachers. The Progressive Caucus was interested foremost in a greatly expanded organizing program for the union. To this end it wanted to build up the national staff and state federations of the AFT. The enlarged national staff would organize new locals and provide services to struggling, small locals that could not provide these services themselves. The Progressive Caucus also wanted to strengthen the national level of the AFT in other ways. For example, part of the caucus program was to establish a full-time legislative representative in Washington, D.C. The caucus wanted to press for federal aid to education. The Progressive Caucus also wanted to establish a prominent journal and it wanted to be active on important national issues. In contrast to the Progressive Caucus, the National Caucus favored strengthening the AFT primarily at the local level. Members of the National Caucus also believed that outside efforts to organize the teachers in a community would usually be fruitless. In their opinion, effective union organizing depended upon the initiative of teachers in a community. Leaders of the National Caucus believed that AFT growth must start in the major cities and then move out from those centers. Indeed, this was the type of growth that had proved successful for the locals in the National Caucus. Traditionally, the large locals had also focused on local political action and local issues.

In a short period of time, during the early 1960s, the issues separating the Progressive Caucus and the National Caucus all but evaporated. The breakthrough in teacher collective bargaining in New York City, similar advances in other cities, extraordinary national membership growth, and new- found power in the political arena presented new challenges and opportunities. A new organizational model emerged among AFT locals which addressed the concerns of both caucuses in the AFT. The union and its locals were able to respond to the local concerns of teachers about students' and teachers' needs, and they were able to influence national issues and national politics. Between 1966 and 1968 the two caucuses, longstanding rivals, merged into one caucus. The leadership and platform of the expanded Progressive Caucus was a smooth blend of the leaders and issue concerns of the former caucuses. However, after the unification of the Progressive Caucus, a series of opposing caucuses emerged. In each instance the opposition caucus was an amalgam of several groups: ultra-leftists, disgruntled local leaders, and groups alleging discrimination. In this rolling, morphing opposition caucus, however, Communist activists of various stripes usually exercised a dominant influence. Some of these activists were holdovers from the earlier Communist-dominated AFT locals aligned with the U.S.S.R. Others were primarily influenced by more recent Communist governments and their policies. A knowledgeable observer could easily discern from their rhetoric and their actions at AFT conventions which part of the East their politics emanate from. Nonetheless, under the consolidated leadership the AFT quickly became one of the largest and most powerful unions in the AFL-CIO.

Bibliography

Appleroth, S. A., and L. D. Edles. 2008. *Classical and Contemporary Sociological Theory: Text and Readings.* Newbury Park, CA: Pine Forge Press.

Bell, D. 1973. *The Coming of Post-Industrial Society.* New York, NY: Basic Books.

Bell, D. 1996. *The Cultural Contradictions of Capitalism.* New York, NY: Basic Books.

Bendix, R. 1977. *Max Weber: An Intellectual Portrait.* Berkeley, CA: University of California Press.

Berube M. R. 2004. *Radical Reformers: The Influence of the Left in American Education.* Charlotte, NC: Information Age Publishing.

Bieger, G. R. "Philosophical Orientations and their Relevance to Education," *JeffBloom.net.*

Blau, P. M., and W. R. Scott. 1962. *Formal Organizations.* San Francisco, CA: Chandler Publishing Company.

Blumer, H. 1954. "What is Wrong with Social Theory," *American Sociological Review* 19(1):3–10.

Blumer, H. 1986. *Symbolic Interaction: Perspective and Method.* Berkeley, CA: University of California Press.

Blumer, H., and T. J. Morrione (editor). 2004. *George Herbert Mead and Human Conduct.* Lanham, MD: AltaMira Press.

Bourdieu, P. 2008. "Legitimation and Structured Interests in Weber's Sociology of Religion," in *Max Weber, Rationality and Modernity*, edited by S. Whimster and S. Lash, 119–136. New York, NY: Routledge, Taylor & Francis Group.

Brekhus, W. 2015. "Lumping and Splitting: Thinking Categorically," in *Cultural Cognition: Patterns in the Social Construction of Reality*, Kindle Edition. Cambridge, England: Polity Press.

Burns, T., and G. L. Stalker. 1994. *The Management of Innovation.* Oxford, England: Oxford University Press.

Bush, G. W. 2006, Dec. 24. Quoted in "The Decider," by S. G. Stolberg, *The New York Times.*

Catropa, D., and M. Andrews. 2013, February 8. "Bemoaning the Corporatization of Higher Education," *Inside Higher Ed—StratEDgy blog.* [https://www.insidehighered.com/blogs/stratedgy/bemoaning-corporatization-higher-education (Accessed 12/24/14)]

Chandler, A. D., Jr. 1993. *Strategy and Structure.* Cambridge, MA: The MIT Press.

Chomsky, N. 2011, April 6. "Academic Freedom and the Corporatization of American Universities," *YouTube.* [www.youtube.com/user/uoftscarborough#p/c/0/Q97tFyqHVLs (Accessed 12/21/15)]

Clark, P. B., and J. Q. Wilson. 1961. Incentive Systems: A Theory of Organizations. *Administrative Science Quarterly,* 6(2).

Clinton, H. 2016. Quoted in "Hillary Clinton's Intersectional Politics," by Clare Foran, *The Atlantic.* [www.theatlantic.com/politics/archive/2016/03/hillary-clinton-intersectionality/472872/ (Accessed 4/17/16)]

Cohen, A., and P. Hamilton (editor). 1985. *The Symbolic Construction of Community.* London, England: Tavistock Books.

Cole, S. 1969. *The Unionization of Teachers.* New York, NY: Praeger Publishers.

Cox, R. W. 2013. The Corporatization of Higher Education. *Class, Race and Corporate Power,* 1(1).

Craig, R. T. 2013. "Constructing theories in communication research," in *Theories and models of communication,* edited by P. Cobley and P. J. Schulz. Berlin, Germany: De Gruyter Mouton.

Crossman, A. "Symbolic Interaction Theory," *About.com Sociology.* [www.thoughtco.com/symbolic-interaction-theory-3026633 (Accessed 3/29/17)]

Dalton, M. 1966. *Men Who Manage.* Hoboken, NJ: John Wiley and Sons.

Davis, K. 1957. *Human Society.* New York, NY: The Macmillan Company.

Delblanco, A. 2017, Sept. 30. "Academic Business," *New York Times Magazine.*

Dewey, J. 1922. *Human Nature and Conduct.* New York, NY: Henry Holt and Company.

Dewey, J. 1929. *Experience and Nature.* Mineola, NY: Dover Publications.

Dewey, J. 1957. *Reconstruction in Philosophy.* Boston, MA: Beacon Press.

Dewey, J. 1961. *Democracy and Education.* New York, NY: The Macmillan Company.

Dewey, J., and J. A. Boydston (editor). 1984. *The Quest for Certainty.* Carbondale, IL: Southern Illinois Press.

Donaldson, L. 1995. *American Anti-Management Theories of Organization.* Cambridge, England: Cambridge University Press.

Durkheim, E. 2014. *The Division of Labor in Society.* New York, NY: Free Press, Simon & Schuster, Inc.

Eisenhower, D. D. 2018, March 6. "Earl Warren," *Wikiquote.* [https://en.wikiquote.org/w/index.php?title=Earl_Warren&oldid=2364952 (Retrieved 3/22/18)]

Eitzen, D. S., and M. B. Zinn. 2001. *Conflict and Order: Understanding Society*. Boston, MA: Allyn and Bacon.

Etzioni, A. 1961. *A Comparative Analysis of Complex Orgnizations*. New York, NY: Free Press, Simon & Schuster, Inc.

Fichtenbaum, R. "Presidential Address," *American Association of University Professors*. [www.aaup.org/news/presidential-address (Accessed 12/21/15a)]

Fichtenbaum, R. "The Corporatization of Higher Education and the Attack on American Workers," PowerPoint Presentation, *American Association of University Professors*. [www.aaupcbc.org (Accessed 12/21/15b)]

Friedman, L. M. Aug 1, 1975. *The Legal System: A Social Science Perspective*. New York, NY: Russell Sage Foundation.

Gouldner, A. W. 1954. *Patterns of Industrial Democracy*. New York, NY: Free Press, Simon & Schuster, Inc.

Grosser, p.E. 1968. *Competitive Interest Group Politics: The Philadelphia Federation of Teachers and the Philadelphia Teachers' Association*. Doctoral Thesis. State College, PA: Penn State University.

Handel, M. J. (editor). 2003. *The Sociology of Organizations: Classic, Contemporary and Critical Readings*. Thousand Oaks, CA: Sage Publications.

Hawley, T. S., A. L. Hostetler, and E. Mooney. 2016. Reconstruction of the fables: The myth of education for democracy, social reconstruction and education for democratic citizenship. *Critical Education*, 7(4).

Hekman, S. 1983. *Weber, the Ideal Type, and Contemporary Social Theory*. Notre Dame, IN: University of Notre Dame Press.

Hendricks, F. 2010. *Vital Democracy: A Theory of Democracy in Action*. Oxford, England: Oxford University Press.

Higgs, S. 2011, Nov. 21. "The Corporatization of the American University," *Counterpunch*. [https://www.counterpunch.org/2011/11/21/the-corporatization-of-the-american-university/ (Accessed 7/12/19)]

Kahlenberg, R. D. 2017. *Tough Liberal: Albert Shanker and the Battles Over Schools, Unions, Race, and Democracy*. New York, NY: Columbia University Press.

Kalberg, S, 1980. Max Weber's Types of Rationality: Cornerstones for the Analysis of Rationalization Processes in History. *American Journal of Sociology*, 85(5).

Kalberg, S. 2012. *Max Weber's Comparative-Historical Sociology Today: Major Themes, Mode of Causal Analysis, and Applications*. Rethinking Classical Sociology (series), Kindle Edition. New York, NY: Routledge, Taylor & Francis Group.

Katz, D., and R. Kahn. 1965. *The Social Psychology of Organizations*. Hoboken, NJ: John Wiley and Sons.

Kaufman, H. 2006. *The Forest Ranger: A Study in Administrative Behavior, Part II, Chapter IV*. New York, NY: Routledge, Taylor & Francis Group.

Keane, F. Dec. 5, 2013. "Obituary: Nelson Mandela," *BBC News*.

King, Martin Luther Jr. 2018, February 18. "Martin Luther King, Jr.," *Wikiquote*. [https://en.wikiquote.org/w/index.php?title=Martin_Luther_King,_Jr.&oldid=2356033 (Retrieved 3/22/18)]

Kyi, A. S. S. 2017, September 26. "Aung San Suu Kyi," *Wikiquote*. [https://en.wikiquote.org/w/index.php?title=Aung_San_Suu_Kyi&oldid=2296516 (Retrieved 3/22/18)]

Lane, J., and K. K. 2015, June 5. "How Universities Turned Themselves Into Global Franchises," *New Republic*.

Lipset, S. M., M. Trow, and J. Coleman. 1962. *Union Democracy*. Garden City, NY: Anchor Books.

Lipset, S. M. 1997. *American Exceptionalism: A Double Edged Sword*. New York, NY: W. W. Norton and Co.

Luxemburg, R., and M. Abidor (translator). 1958. "In the Storm," *Le Socialiste*, May 1904.

MacArthur, D. 2018, March 21. "Douglas MacArthur," *Wikiquote*. [https://en.wikiquote.org/w/index.php?title=Douglas_MacArthur&oldid=2373207 (Retrieved 3/22/18)]

March, J. G., and H. A. Simon. 1958. *Organizations*. Hoboken, NJ: John Wiley and Sons.

Marx, K. A. 1977. *Contribution to the Critique of Political Economy*. Moscow, Russia: Progress Publishers.

McClelland, D. C. 1961. *The Achieving Society*. New York, NY: D. Van Nostrand Company, Inc.

McGregor, D. 1976. *The Human Side of Enterprise*. New York, NY: McGraw-Hill.

Mead, G. H., and A. E. Murphy (editor). 1932. *The Philosophy of the Present*. Chicago, IL: University of Chicago Press.

Mead, G. H., and A. J. Reck (editor). 1964. *Selected Writings: George Herbert Mead*. Chicago, IL: Phoenix Books, University of Chicago Press.

Mead, G. H., and C. W. Morris (editor). 1965a. *Mind, Self, and Society*. Chicago, IL: University of Chicago Press.

Mead, G. H., and A. Strauss (editor). 1965b. *George Herbert Mead on Social Psychology*. Chicago, IL: Phoenix Books, University of Chicago Press.

Mead, G. H., and C. W. Morris (editor). 1972a. *The Philosophy of the Act*. Chicago, IL: University of Chicago Press.

Mead, G. H., and M. H. Moore (editor). 1972b. *Movements of Thought in the Nineteenth Century*. Chicago, IL: University of Chicago Press.

Mead, G. H., and F. Carreira da Silva (editor). 2011. *Mead: A Reader*. New York, NY: Routledge, Taylor & Francis Group.

Miller, D. L. 1973. *George Herbert Mead: Self, Language and the World*. Austin, TX: University of Texas Press.

Mills, C. W. 1961. *The Sociological Imagination*. New York, NY: Grove Press.

Mills, N. 2012. "The Corporatization of Higher Education," *Dissent*, Fall.

Morris, G. D. 1977. *Teachers and Union Democracy*. Doctoral Thesis. Cambridge, MA: Harvard University.

Mortensen, T. G. 2012, Winter. "State Funding: A Race to the Bottom," *American Council on Education*.

Mansbridge, J. J. 1990. *Beyond Self Interest*. Chicago, IL: University of Chicago Press.

Murrow, S. E. 2011. Depicting Teachers' Roles in Social Reconstruction in the Social Frontier, 1934–1943. *Education Theory*, 61(3).

Ouchi, W. 1981. *Theory Z: How American Business Can Meet the Japanese Challenge*. Boston, MA: Addison-Wesley Publishing Company, Inc.

Parsons, T. 1947. *Max Weber: The Theory of Social and Economic Organization*. Oxford, England: Oxford University Press.

Pascale, C.-M. 2010. "Chapter Four: Symbolic Interaction," in *Cartographies of Knowledge: Exploring Qualitative Epistemologies*. Thousand Oaks, CA: Sage Publications.

Perrow, C. 1986. *Complex Organizations: A Critical Essay*. New York, NY: McGraw-Hill.

Pope John XXIII, *Mater et Magistra, Encyclical of Pope John XXIII on Christianity and Social Progress*, May 15, 1961. [www.papalencyclicals.net/john23/j23mater.htm (Accessed 7/17/13)]

Popper, K. 1989. *The Poverty of Historicism*. London, England: Ark Paperbacks.

Ritzer, G. 2000. *The McDonaldization of Society*. Newbury Park, CA: Pine Forge Press.

Roosevelt, T. 2018, January 18. "Theodore Roosevelt," *Wikiquote*. [https://en.wikiquote.org/w/index.php?title=Theodore_Roosevelt&oldid=2341247 (Retrieved 3/22/18)]

Rosenthal, G. 2012. "More Empirical and More Historical Sociology," in *The Shape of Sociology for the 21st Century: Tradition and Renewal*, edited by D. Kalikin-Fishman and A. Denis. Thousand Oaks, CA: Sage Publications.

Schmidlin, K. 2015, October 10. "The corporatization of higher education: With a system that caters to the 1 percent, students and faculty get screwed," *Salon*. [www.salon.com/2015/10/10/the_corporatization_of_higher_education_with_a_system_that_caters_to_the_1_percent_students_and_faculty_get_screwed/ (Accessed 12/24/15)]

Schuman, R. 2014. "Syllabus Tyrannus," *Slate*. [www.slate.com/articles/life/education/2014/08/college_course_syllabi_they_re_too_long_and_they_re_a_symbol_of_the_decline.html (Accessed 12/29/15)]

Scott, W. R. 1998. *Organizations: Rational, Natural, and Open Systems*. Upper Saddle River, NJ: Prentice Hall.

Selznick, p.1966. *TVA and the Grass Roots*. New York, NY: Harper Torchbooks.

Shibutani, T. 1955. Reference Groups as Perspectives. *American Journal of Sociology*, 60(6).

Shils, E. 1965. Charisma, Order, and Status. *American Sociological Review*, 30(2).

Simon, H. 1997 (1957). *Administrative Behavior*. New York, NY: Free Press, Simon & Schuster, Inc.

Stanford University. H. 2017, Nov 27 (2007, Aug 24). "Max Weber," by S. H. Kim, in the *Stanford Encyclopedia of Philosophy*. [https://plato.stanford.edu/entries/weber/, pp. 11-12, August 24, 2007 (Accessed 4/12/16)]

Stark, W. 1991. *The Sociology of Knowledge: Towards a Deeper Understanding of the History of Ideas*. New Brunswick, NJ: Transaction Publishers.

Strauss A. L., L. Schatzman, R. Bucher, D. Ehrlich, and M. Sabshin. 1963. "The Hospital and Its Negotiated Order," in *Hospital in Modern Society*, edited by E. Freidson. New York, NY: Free Press, Simon & Schuster, Inc.

Stryker, S. 1981. "Symbolic Interactionism: Themes and Variations," in *Social Psychology: Sociological Perspectives*, edited by M. Rosenberg and R. H. Turner. New York, NY: Basic Books.

Swedberg, R. 2005. *The Max Weber Dictionary*. Palo Alto, CA: Stanford University Press.

Teryakian, E. A. 1965. Existential Sociology and the Sociological Tradition. *American Sociological Review*, 30(5).

Thomas, W. I., and D. S. Thomas. 1928. *The Child in America*. New York, NY: Alfred A. Knopf, Inc.

Tonnies, F. 2011. *Community and Society*. Mineola, NY: Dover Publications.

Watson, E. 2018, January 6. "Emma Watson," *Wikiquote*. [https://en.wikiquote.org/w/index.php?title=Emma_Watson&oldid=2335145 (Retrieved 3/22/18)]

Weber, M., H. H. Gerth and C. W. Mills (translators). 1946. *From Max Weber*. Oxford, England: Oxford University Press.

Weber, M., G. Roth and C. Wittich (editors) 1978. *Economy and Society*. Berkeley, CA: University of California Press.

Weber, M. 1993. *Basic Concepts in Sociology*. New York, NY: Citadel Press.

Weber, M. 1987. *The Protestant Ethic and the Spirit of Capitalism*. London, England: Unwin Paperbacks, Allen & Unwin.

Westheimer, J. 2010, April. "Higher Education or Education for Hire? Corporatization and the Threat to Democratic Thinking," *Academic Matters*. [https://academicmatters.ca/higher-education-or-education-for-hire-corporatization-and-the-threat-to-democratic-thinking/ (Accessed 7/12/19)]

Wilson, J. Q. 1995. *Political Organizations*. Princeton, NJ: Princeton University Press.

X, M. 2018, February 28. "Malcolm X," *Wikiquote*. [https://en.wikiquote.org/w/index.php?title=Malcolm_X&oldid=2361950 (Retrieved 3/22/18)]